# King's Speech

For T'Iona:

Peace & Justice

Truth "is" love ...

Gunggu Dr. 20. 2020

# King's Speech

Preaching Reconciliation in a
World of Violence and Chasm

*Sunggu Yang*

FOREWORD BY
*Rebecca Hernandez*

 CASCADE *Books* · Eugene, Oregon

KING'S SPEECH
Preaching Reconciliation in a World of Violence and Chasm

Cascade Books
An Imprint of Wipf and Stock Publishers
199 W. 8th Ave., Suite 3
Eugene, OR 97401

www.wipfandstock.com

PAPERBACK ISBN: 978-1-5326-5091-8
HARDCOVER ISBN: 978-1-5326-5092-5
EBOOK ISBN: 978-1-5326-5093-2

*Cataloguing-in-Publication data:*

Names: Yang, Sunggu, 1980–, author. | Hernandez, Rebecca, foreword.

Title: King's speech : preaching reconciliation in a world of violence and
chasm / Sunggu Yang ; foreword by Rebecca Hernandez.

Description: Eugene, OR : Cascade Books, 2019 | Includes bibliographical
references and index.

Identifiers: ISBN 978-1-5326-5091-8 (paperback) | ISBN 978-1-5326-5092-5
(hardcover) | ISBN 978-1-5326-5093-2 (ebook)

Subjects: LCSH: King, Martin Luther,—Jr.,—1929–1968. | King, Martin
Luther,—Jr.,—1929–1968—Oratory. | Preaching.

Classification: BV4208.U6 Y36 2019 (print) | BV4208.U6 Y36 (ebook)

Manufactured in the U.S.A.                                    MAY 20, 2019

*To Dale*
*Beloved Teacher*

# Contents

# Foreword

SERMONS HAVE ALWAYS MADE a difference in my life to encourage, console, correct, inspire, teach the good way, and avoid the bad. In my world, my pastors were Latino like me, and helped raise us in our little Spanish-speaking church. They not only preached Good News, but also served to motivate and engage us to act for the good of the community, for the people who were suffering injustice. This was common, and we would spend hours in prayer and then hours working for the poor and less fortunate.

Although I later learned we were thought of as the poorest and least fortunate by virtue of our ethnicity and our geographic location, we stood in prayer for others who went through severe domestic abuse, those who were cheated from their wages, and for ourselves, students who constantly faced temptations, challenges, and discrimination in schools. Growing up, the words of God challenged the status quo and provided ultimate hope that shaped my worldview, which in turn has shaped my calling and work today.

I currently serve as the Chief Diversity Officer and Associate Provost of Local and Global Engagement at George Fox University. This role of Chief Diversity Officer, while not as unique in institutions of higher learning as it once was, is still a fairly new position in Christian Higher Education. It's a role that many feel we don't need because we have Jesus, and he calls us to love everyone and so we don't "see" color, race, or difference. Sadly, we know that's not true, and while we hope and pray for more unity in the church, our history has not borne that out.

Dr. King's life and work was about this love of God for *all* his people, black, Latino, Asian, and all others. As noted by the author of this book, Dr. Yang, King was first a preacher. His task of taking God's word and making meaning for us through preaching is a weighty task, which King did brilliantly. This was done not with complicated theological words but with simple truth, love, and a call for those who listened to love others and pursue justice. The ability to inspire others, to encourage others through the Word of God is one of the most sacred and powerful gifts. King had that gift then and still does now.

I have been moved by King's sermons along with those of my own pastors to do something, to live out my life in service of justice and reconciliation—first as a teacher, researcher, faculty member, and now as an administrator. One of my responsibilities is to oversee the work of the Center for Peace and Justice. As I now direct this spirited center at George Fox University, I resonate even more with the holy words I heard as a youth. Our work, like many similar centers, is to highlight the good news of peace, justice, and reconciliation through academic study and organized engagement of students, faculty, and others to discuss and to develop ways to fulfill the call of Christ as peacemaker. I often look back to the words of Dr. King that call us to be peacemakers and to seek justice and mercy for ourselves and for others. It is a challenging time to call out for this peace, but it is also necessary today as then.

King was also situated in a very challenging time. The civil rights movement about which he writes and preaches was met with hatred and violence by many Americans and even opposition from those who would call themselves Christians. Today looks very much like those days. Even while I am writing this, our country is recovering from the murder of African Americans because they were African American in Kentucky, the killing of Jews during a service in a synagogue, and the mistreatment of migrants detained in inhumane situations who have been torn from their children. The list could go on. Strife and hate seem to rule the day, but we know there is much more that needs to be said, to be done, to counter these messages, and I wonder who can speak into this void. I am pleased to say that Dr. King's words ring as true today as they did when they were written. Who better to champion the cause of the vulnerable and to call out the Christians who at times seem more like enemies than brothers or sisters?

In this book, Dr. Yang lays out the history of Dr. King's evolution as a thoughtful theologian who was raised in the black church tradition, yet incorporated new knowledge constantly as he grew as a leader and preacher. The discussion continues into the understanding of the role of King as the preacher who not only proclaimed the Word of justice and love from the pulpit of a church building, but also from the "street pulpit" and the prison. Throughout the book, Dr. Yang shows how effectively, powerfully, and bravely King advocated the cause of the vulnerable and called out the Christians to actions through his preaching ministry.

I am grateful to Dr. Yang, a scholar of homiletics and Asian-American Christianity, to name but a few of his areas of expertise. Dr. Yang is well qualified to write on and share about King's great work. But for me, I was struck by his deep love of the Word when he shared a story with me about how he would often preach at a little church with a small, aging congregation. His excitement as he recounted the experience demonstrated his deep love and appreciation for the practice of preaching—the gift that good, clear sharing of the Word of God has for those who listen. I have been blessed to know Dr. Yang as he serves in our Christian Studies department and teaches homiletics and the Bible. Our students are blessed to have Dr. Yang and his remarkable work on King.

I encourage you, with this book, to take a deep dive into the sermons and life of Dr. King, whose message is as relevant today as it was over fifty years ago. We know the Word of God is for us today, and through anointed preaching, it gives life, comfort, and inspiration. Let these words inspire and move your heart to action.

Rebecca Hernandez, PhD
Chief Diversity Officer
Director, Center for Peace & Justice
George Fox University

# Preface

In 2018, as we celebrate the fiftieth anniversary of Rev. Dr. Martin Luther King Jr.'s tragic assassination in 1968, we increasingly feel the need for his presence among us. News, incidents, and rumors of racism are reported across the country while bloody terror, hatred, and new schisms headline most media outlets daily. People live in constant fear and animosity, not knowing who is going to do what, when—it could be a friend, neighbor, nation, or international most-wanted. So, we readily shut ourselves up, constructing our own hidden ghettos, both physically and psychologically, never daring to welcome any "others" into the midst of our false havens. Do we have any hope? Are there any words of hope? Where is that audacious preacher of hope to be found?

Preacher King was a figure of hope for his time, and thankfully, for ours as well. His enduring wisdom and words of peace and reconciliation remind us time and again that there is eternal power and impeccable hope in God, in whose infinite love we find the strength to love and restore this broken world. King knew that wherever there is hatred, we can still sow respect and friendship; wherever there is terror, we can still express good will and kindness; and wherever there is prejudice, we can still break down walls of separation. Do these sacred tasks still look impossible and idealistic? Yes, they do. Yet, as King encourages, remember that "only in the darkness can we see the stars."

I write this focused book on King's preaching in order to help the reader navigate and apply his timeless message of peace, forgiveness, and reconciliation to this modern world of despair and disappointment. For this purpose, we will read various sermon excerpts from King, given that his most important theology of reconciliation and spiritual force are found primarily in his sermons. As he himself acknowledged, he appeared most impactful, hopeful, and spirited when he stood at the pulpit with the holy words.

The primary audience of this work will be mainstream professionals (e.g., seminary students in courses on prophetic preaching or students of peace and reconciliation studies). For this reason, I aim to avoid—as much as possible—theological jargon and lengthy discussions on academic minutiae, in an attempt to make this work easily accessible. Prophetic pastors and faith leaders in social ministry will find in this book easy access to King's profound ideas on violence and reconciliation for their own meaning-making in many different contexts of conflict and division today. General readers interested in King's legacy on the social reconciliation movement will find here many practical and ethical lessons they can adopt in their own situations.

Finally, I express my gratitude to my editor, Dr. Charlie Collier at Wipf and Stock Publishers who put his trust in this book project and guided me in numerous ways throughout the production and completion of the book. My special thanks go to Prof. Dale P. Andrews and Prof. Leonora Tubbs Tisdale whose prophetic preaching classes years ago first drew me into the works of King. At the end of the book, the reader will find in an appendix a sermon I wrote years ago in Tisdale's class and revised for publication—a sermon written in inspiration of King. I do hope many will also be inspired by King to write and speak their own prophetic messages. Last, but not least, I have to thank my student assistant Tanner Nicholls at George Fox University, whose research support and copyediting has been invaluable during this book's final stage of production.

More words of gratitude to many should be said. But, let me stop. My only real intention at this point is to prepare the way for King. Let him speak more. It's time to be challenged and encouraged by him once again.

# Introduction

> I am many things to many people. But in the quiet re-
> cesses of my heart, I am fundamentally a clergyman, a
> Baptist preacher. This is my being and my heritage, for
> I am also the son of a Baptist preacher, the grandson of
> a Baptist preacher and the great-grandson of a Baptist
> preacher.[1]

No other statement could identify King better than this. Thus,
this statement is the launching point for this research on preacher
King's theology on violence and reconciliation. Admittedly, there
already exists a wealth of research regarding King's theology, social
gospel, civil rights movements, ethics, philosophical backgrounds,
personal convictions, and so forth.[2] These efforts to explore King's
Christian identity and social legacy have produced a great deal of
helpful academic as well as practical results. However, as long as
we acknowledge that King himself was fundamentally a preacher,
we come to recognize that these aforementioned efforts have inevitable limits in understanding King and investigating his legacy.
More explicitly, King can be best understood only when we con-
sider him as a preacher with his own preaching theology. Hence,
this research attempts to understand King and his legacy in light of
his unique theology of preaching on violence and reconciliation.
As noted, a considerable number of studies that deal with King's

1. King, "The UnChristian Christian," 76.

2. See Garrow, *Bearing the Cross*; Ansbro, *Martin Luther King, Jr.*; Baldwin,
*There is a Balm in Gilead*; Bellah, *The Broken Covenant*; Oates, *Let the Trumpet
Sound*, and many others.

theology in general—particularly in relation to black church traditions—have already been conducted. However, that approach has been too broad and, at times, vague. Researching his preaching theology, I contend, is a more targetable approach. This is because King was not fundamentally a systematic theologian, an ethicist, or a social activist, but a preacher.

Ultimately, this research will show that in his preaching King realizes and propagates the God of cosmic reconciliation manifested through(out) the universe. This same being groans over all types of violence happening in the human world as God, the creator and sustainer of the universal moral law, also personally relates to all humanity. Here the concept of God relating to *all* humanity is important. Since God relates personally to *all*, God's universal love is also extended to all the immoral, the wicked, the violent, the oppressors, or "the enemies" as King would call them. The universal and personal God initiates great (indeed, unimaginable) reconciliation in the midst of immoral violence toward the establishment of the "Beloved Community." Bluntly put, the oppressed and the oppressors together become God's beloved without hate, prejudice, exploitation, or death. Admittedly, this is a hard lesson on both sides. The oppressed demand retribution while the oppressors will not yield their position of power and associated privileges anytime soon. But, King is aware that in order for this uneasy lesson to be seen as practical, people will require a demonstration—an example. For King, that demonstration is Christ's sacrifice upon the cross. Impossible became possible in and through him. Thus, the hard lesson has now become a desired one for all to follow.

With this elaborate theology, King vitalizes a pastoral *and* prophetic preaching voice that seeks peace and reconciliation in the context of a violent reality. Indeed, it is quite fair to say that King's pastoral and prophetic preaching develops that reconciliatory theology. King didn't write a single systematic theology book, yet his preaching was his theology. It is like proving the old famous liturgical saying, *lex orandi, lex credendi,* which can be loosely translated as, "The law of preaching is the law of believing."[3] Given

3. The most adopted translation is "The law of praying is the law of

that preaching is at the center of King's theological formation, the book will proceed in the following order:

- Chapter 1: Backgrounds of King's Preaching Theology. This chapter traces various historical and intellectual influences on the development of King's critical thoughts on God, evil, humanity, the church, society, morality, preaching, and more. The three sub-sections of the chapter show specific ecclesial, academic, and socio-cultural influences on King: (1) The influence of the black church tradition; (2) the influence of contemporary theologies (specifically those of his black theological background, his intellectual experiences at Morehouse College, theological developments at Crozer Seminary, new philosophical encounters at Boston University, and finally theological influences from Paul Tillich and Karl Barth); and (3) the environment of violence, both societal-physical and spiritual-moral, in which King lived.

- Chapter 2: King's God Manifested through the Universe and Violent Reality. Based on various historical and intellectual influences discussed in chapter 1, King develops his own theological thoughts on God, humanity, Jesus, the universe, and evil. Finally, his imperative thoughts on violence and universal reconciliation emerge. This chapter studies how King further develops and incarnates his theological reflections on violence and reconciliation in his sermons and various writings like "The Letter from Birmingham Jail." A mark of King's greatness is his creativity and capacity to make abstract theological ideas easily accessible and applicable (for life) in his sermons and writings.

- Chapter 3: Invention of Other-Typological Illustration in Preaching. This chapter takes the reader deep into the homiletical world of preacher King. Through a close analysis of

believing." This means that it is the prayer which leads to belief or that it is liturgy which leads to theology. Preaching as a crucial part of liturgy, we may say, then leads to theology, thus legitimizing the phrase, "The law of preaching is the law of believing."

one of King's famous sermons, the chapter shows how King strategically crafts his sermon in order to maximize the impact of his thoughts about violence and reconciliation. The sermon analyzed is, "Death of Evil upon the Seashore" as preached at the Cathedral of St. John the Divine in New York City on May 17, 1956.

• Chapter 4: King Still Speaking to the Violent World Today. Every January when we celebrate MLK Jr. Day, we are easily aware that his spiritual, moral, and social legacy still breathes around us today. This chapter briefly discusses three concrete lessons from King's preaching life around his profound notion of the "Beloved Community."

In the end, I hope my readers keep one thing in mind: this book is not a book on King's theology, but an enthusiastic glimpse into King's *theological preaching*. Hence, throughout the book we will read many of King's sermons and sermonic writings from various points in his life and how they manifest King's theology. I do hope that we all hear again King's unique visionary voice enriched with his thick revolutionary theology. This focused hearing, I believe, will encourage us to live boldly and continue his historical legacy of reconciliatory work in today's world of terror and fear. There is truly a good reason why we need to hear King's speech once again. Surely, after fifty years, King still speaks among us. Can't you still hear him?

# 1

## Backgrounds of King's Preaching Theology

### The Influence of the Black Church Tradition

FROM BIRTH, KING WAS surrounded and influenced by the black faith community. Both his maternal grandfather and his father were successful African-American Baptist preachers in Atlanta, Georgia. Put simply, "King was a product of the black church in America."[1] How exactly, then, did the black Baptist church—or the black church in general—influence King's reconciliatory preaching theology? There are at least three significant elements of the black church tradition that influenced King: the freedom tradition, open-ended Christian practices, and the particular interpretative tools of allegory and typology.

First is the black church's "freedom tradition." Long before the birth of King, black people had been singing hymns such as the one below:

> Children, we all shall be free
> When the Lord shall appear![2]

1. Lischer, *Preacher King*, 5.
2. Southern and Wright, *African-American Traditions*, 37.

And,

> Oh Freedom, Oh Freedom, Oh Freedom over me!
> Before I'll be a slave
> I'll be buried in my grave,
> And go home to my Lord
> And be free.[3]

And,

> In Christ now meet both east and west,
>     In Him meet south and north:
> All Christly souls are one in Him
>     Throughout the whole wide earth.[4]

As seen in the songs above, a fundamental motif of freedom and liberation permeated black Christians' lives from their first exposure to Christianity in America. They found both spiritual enhancement for their oppressed lives and eschatological hope by singing and dreaming of their own liberation from oppression. In fact, it was none other than this spiritual enhancement and eschatological hope that propelled early African-American Christians to walk out of the churches of white slave owners and start black churches. The African Methodist Episcopal Church (A.M.E.) in 1787 was the first example of such a walkout. Richard Allen, founder and first consecrated bishop of the A.M.E. church, departed from St. George's Methodist Church in Philadelphia, Pennsylvania, and started the first African-American denomination.[5]

By the time of King's birth, black Christians in America had already been actively engaging in social movements to improve black lives and, therefore, most black churches in America functioned as both spiritual homes and social-movement base camps.[6]

---

3. *African American Heritage Hymnal*, 545.

4. *African American Heritage Hymnal*, 399.

5. Abington, *Readings*, 30.

6. However, not all black churches were part of the civil rights movement. Indeed, there were a considerable number of black churches that did not participate in the movement, and rather took an accommodationist position.

So, it comes as no surprise that King was surrounded and influenced by this spiritual and social ethos while being raised as a pastor's son. Consequently, it was deeply rooted in King's mind, theological thoughts, and preaching from his childhood. When King was led to public service, that ethos was evidently present in his preaching and various speeches, as we can see in the following excerpt:

> It seemed as though I could hear the quiet assurance of an inner voice, saying, "Stand up for righteousness, stand up for truth. God will be at your side forever." . . . Let this affirmation be our ringing cry. It will give us courage to face the uncertainties of the future. It will give our tired feet new strength as we continue our forward stride toward the city of freedom. When our days become dreary with low-hovering clouds and our nights become darker than a thousand midnights, let us remember that there is a great benign Power in the universe whose name is God, and he is able to make a way out of no way, and transform dark yesterdays into bright tomorrows.[7]

These words sound almost like the lyrics of an old-time black spiritual, which evidently proves King's inheritance of the black church's freedom and liberation tradition.

The second influential element on King's preaching is that of the black church's open-ended Christian practices. These practices include extending biblical narratives into the church's own worldly experience, performing Scripture in its music, its rhythmic pattern

---

Hans Baer and Merrill Singer explain this in their book, *African American Religion: Varieties of Protest and Accommodation*. Through thorough research on African-American mainstream churches, Messianic-nationalist sects, conversionist sects, thaumaturgical sects, etc. in the twentieth century, they find not only that there have been varieties of social protest in the black church, but also that there were varieties of accommodationist positions in the black church, influenced in particular by advanced industrial capitalism. Thus, at this point it would not be correct to say that all black churches in the early or middle twentieth century were active participants in social or civil rights transformation.

7. King, *Strength to Love*, 114.

of call and response, and rhetorical adornments.[8] Richard Lischer observes that all of these are techniques that King "exported from the church's Sunday worship to political mass meetings around the country."[9] Quite understandably, these practices enabled King to find God revealed and speaking through the whole universe, that is, both sacred and secular realms. Above all, extending the Bible into the church's own worldly experience affirms God's universal reign in the world. Performing the Scripture in music creates the Scripture's common virtue in the secular world thanks to the universality of music itself. And black worship's pattern of call and response enables people's active engagement with divinity, whether the listeners are Christian or not (therefore, universal engagement!), by appealing to human beings' most common desire for communication with each other and with the divine. Lastly, various rhetorical adornments help King inflate "local conflicts into the titanic battle of universals."[10] With the underlying influence of the black church's open-ended practices, King was able to transform "the Judeo-Christian themes of love, suffering, deliverance, and justice from the sacred shelter of the pulpit into the arena of public policy."[11]

Thirdly, King's theology was informed by the black church's interpretative tools of allegory and typology. Regarding this matter, Lischer says:

> [T]hey [allegory and typology] allowed his congregations a greater opportunity to identify their struggles with those portrayed in the Bible. The black church not only sought to locate truth *in* the Bible, in order to derive lessons from it, but also extended the Bible its own experience. King found the ancient methods of interpretation useful in his effort to enroll the Civil Rights Movement in the saga of divine revelation.[12]

8. Lischer, *Preacher King*, 7.

9. Lischer, *Preacher King*, 7.

10. Lischer, *Preacher King*, 9.

11. Lischer, *Preacher King*, 4.

12. Lischer, *Preacher King*, 7.

What is evident in Lischer's observation is that by utilizing the interpretative tools of the black church's tradition, King succeeded in intertwining the realm of divine revelation with the secular realm, wherein the civil rights movement is perceived as a divine claim. In doing so, King eventually came to confront the God revealed through the whole universe again and again.

King was a product of the black church, and his own theological identity was deeply influenced by the black church tradition. Specifically, King found his God revealed through the whole universe as a result of the three major influences of the tradition that we discussed above. However, the influence from the black church was not enough for King to develop his own homiletic theology, which he needed in order to confront the cruel reality of the America in which he lived. He needed more than influence itself. He needed a deeper articulation of the human condition, a broad and comprehensive understanding of God, and his own homiletic voice to confront this violent reality. As one can guess, all of these higher disciplines came from his advanced theological studies. Therefore, it is now time to turn to King's theological background and how it deepened his understanding of theology and preaching of reconciliation.

## The Influence from Contemporary Theologies

King went through three influential academic institutions: Morehouse, Crozer Seminary, and Boston University (where he wrote his dissertation in theology). These institutions gradually helped King to develop his own prophetic voice, which would echo God revealed or manifested through the universe during his public life. In particular, significant influence on King's preaching theology came from King's contemporary theologians, such as Benjamin E. Mays, George W. Davis, and Boston Personalist theologians like Harold DeWolf, along with Paul Tillich and Karl Barth in whose works King had a vast interest. Besides, King had been largely influenced by black theological legacies he inherited from his Ebenezer church experience and his active participation in black theology. Hence, this section investigates the theological influences mentioned above, including the homiletic influence of black theological legacies.[13] It is perhaps best for us to start with King's black theological legacies, since those legacies are the fundamental theological ground of King's experience and development as an African American preacher and practical theologian. From here, we will move on to explore his major intellectual sources.

### Black Theological Ground

It is quite difficult to trace the exact black theological legacies King inherited. This is partly because King did not have a chance to be educated under black academic theologians (instead his experience of black theology was observed from influential black preachers[14]), and also because his main theological interest was not in the black theological tradition. Even his doctoral dissertation was about two white theologians' conceptions of God. Nonetheless, it is not impossible to explore the influence black theology had on King's homiletic theology, thanks to the works of some prominent black theologians such as James H. Cone, Noel L. Erskine, and specifically Richard Lischer's outstanding research on King's preaching and theology.[15] The two former theologians do not specifically deal with King's preaching theology. Nevertheless, their articulation of King's black theology, and its theological implications for

13. This investigation will help us understand how these various theological influences contribute particularly to the formation of King's homiletic theology of reconciliation and ecumenism. Admittedly, this is not the only way to read these influences. William D. Watley reads them as the formative sources of King's evangelical socialism, while Kenneth L. Smith and Ira G. Zepp Jr. read them as the intellectual sources of King's evangelical ethical ideals. Recently, Richard Wayne Will Sr. identified them as the critical sources of Kingian doctrines of God. See Watley, *Roots of Resistance*; Smith and Zepp, *Search for the Beloved Community*; and Wills, *Martin Luther King Jr. and the Image of God*. For the purpose of the project, however, this investigation intentionally focuses on the theological sources' influences on King's homiletic imagination and theology.

14. Lischer, *Preacher King*, 15–37.

15. Their publications will be at times quoted later in this study.

King's life and work, provides essential theological accounts. Thus, I will call upon these important research efforts to explore King's black theological foundations.

First, we need to investigate what practical and fundamental theological legacy King inherited from his home church, Ebenezer Baptist. "The church," King recalls in his autobiography of religious development, "has always been a second home for me."[16] It is obvious that Ebenezer was the place that provided his early religious experience and formed his basic theological concerns. According to Lischer, Ebenezer Baptist Church had considerable influence on King at least in three ways that this project will later articulate and develop in relation to King's own homiletic and theological ideas of God, humanity, and the universe.

First, at his home church King experienced a God who is all powerful, ever present, and ceaselessly loving.[17] Being taught along fundamentalist lines in the black Baptist church,[18] King formed his own religious universe with an omnipotent, omniscient, and all-loving God—even though he later confessed in an autobiographical statement to "removing the shackles of fundamentalism."[19]

The church's second theological influence on King was its active social concern.[20] King's congregation recognized a God who

16. Garrow, *Martin Luther King, Jr.*, 361.

17. Lischer, *Preacher King*, 15–17.

18. Garrow, *Martin Luther King, Jr.*, 359–62. King uses the often historically loaded term "fundamentalism" to mean 1) the infallibility of Scriptures and thus the invalidation of historical biblical criticism, 2) evangelistic conversion of an individual, 3) belief in the bodily resurrection of Jesus, and 4) a patriarchal understanding of God and the pastorate. King later came to seriously revise this fundamentalist view as he acquired a more liberal theological education at Crozer seminary and Boston University.

19. Carson, Luker, and Russell, *Papers*, 363.

20. Indeed, it wasn't just Ebenezer Baptist Church but its pastor, King's father, that influenced King's lifetime social concern. Already, "decades earlier to the Montgomery bus boycott, King's activist father [along with the church] refused to commute on a segregated bus system, fought for parity in teacher salaries, and desegregated courthouse elevators" (Wills, *Image of God*, 33). Thus, it is no surprise that King confesses, "My admiration of him [the father] was a great moving factor; he set forth a noble example that I didn't mind following" (King, "An Autobiography of Religious Development [1950]," in *The Papers*, 1:360).

was actively working to transform black people's oppressed status, and the church was believed to be a vehicle for that divine act. To put it more theologically, "King's congregation knew that the future of the Kingdom of God [eschatological hope] was meant to be seen and tasted in *this* life."[21] Hence, it was very natural that when he arrived in Atlanta years later to serve his home church, "King linked the salvation of the church to the economic and social health of the Negro in Atlanta."[22]

Lastly, the faith experience at Ebenezer church provided King with an image of what a preacher ought to be, which King later reflected throughout his public life. Regarding this matter, Lischer writes, "At Ebenezer, young King learned that when the preacher assumes his proper place in hierarchy above the people and beneath the cross—and says what God wants him to say—the entire organism hums with celestial power. The people had better pay attention."[23] In Lischer's observation, two things are very clear: (1) God is continuously in dialogue with humans and specifically gives the Word to the preacher, and (2) when the preacher preaches, the whole universe helps the preacher to deliver God's word. These fundamental beliefs were paramount when King was in the public eye, since they legitimized King as a preacher of the universally speaking God for the sake of the oppressed.

In sum, Ebenezer Baptist planted the seeds of King's future evangelical social service. There he found the God and the Word upon whom he would call in his public service, formed his basic worldview, and became aware of his own identity as a public preacher.

Regarding King's preaching and theology, James Cone writes, "It is to his credit that he never allowed a pietistic faith in the other world to become a substitute for good judgment in this world. He not only preached sermons about the Promised Land

21. Lischer, *Preacher King*, 17.

22. Lischer, *Preacher King*, 24.

23. Lischer, *Preacher King*, 17.

but concretized his vision with a political attempt to actualize his hope."[24] And in 1969, the National Committee of Black Churchmen stated:

> Black theology is a theology of liberation. It seeks to plumb the black condition in the light of God's revelation in Jesus Christ, so that the black community can see that the gospel is commensurate with the achievement of black community. Black theology is a theology of "blackness." It is the affirmation of black community that emancipates black people from white racism, thus providing authentic freedom for both white and black people. It affirms the humanity of white people in that it says no to the encroachment of white oppression.[25]

In the statements above, we find two important black theological ideas that colored King's homiletic theology.

First, as black theology does, most of King's preaching seeks liberation of the oppressed in *this* world, rather than only in the world to come. From its inception, black theology has been a theology of liberation.[26] It eagerly sought to liberate theology from dominant white American and European theology and to free the oppressed, in particular black people, from social, religious, economic, and political oppression.[27] Although King did not

24. Erskine, *King among the Theologians*, 122.

25. Wilmore and Cone, *Black Theology*, 101. There is, indeed, a caveat to this statement: in historical terms, we must recognize the statement as an appeal for black theology to *become* what it describes. In other words, black theologians in this period were bringing this form of liberation theology into existence, not simply describing a black theology that had always existed. This is not to say that black theologians before this time did not have similar analyses—theologians and church leaders such as Reverdy Ransom, Howard Thurman, and others certainly did. However, the specific formulation of a "theology of liberation" was new in this period, in that it came after (and in many ways was a result of) the civil rights movement, and cannot be taken as an ahistorical description of what black theology had always been—or, for that matter, of what all black theology has been since that time.

26. Cone, *For My People*, 53.

27. As discussed briefly above, in King's time, the formulation of black theology as a theology of liberation was in the beginning stage. Further, King did

ultimately succeed in this theology of total liberation, he none-theless took the idea seriously and incorporated it into his own homiletic theology. In fact, this was a natural development of his theology, since most of his preaching and speeches were delivered in the public arena for the real (or practical) sake of the oppressed. King preaches:

> I say to you that our goal is freedom, and I believe we are going to get there because however much she strays away from it, the goal of America is freedom. Abused and scorned though we may be as a people, our destiny is tied up in the destiny of America . . . If the inexpress-ible cruelties of slavery couldn't stop us, the opposition that we now face will surely fail. We're going to win our freedom because both the sacred heritage of our nation and the eternal will of the almighty are embodied in our echoing demands.[28]

Clearly, King's target is *America, here and now*. This tangible worldly reality must go through liberation and transformation.

Second, as black theology seeks the reconciliation of the op-pressed and the oppressors, King's preaching also echoes the idea of reconciliation between blacks and whites.[29] In fact, the ultimate

---

not understand himself as a liberation theologian, a term that did not exist in the 1950s and early 1960s. Thus, it would suffice here to state that King helped inspire the work of the black liberation theological movement rather than that he adopted a fully-fledged liberation theology.

28. Carson and Holloran, *A Knock at Midnight*, 222–23.

29. King's ideal of reconciliation toward or beyond liberation did not go without criticism from contemporary black theologians and liberation so-cialists. In particular, the prominent Muslim liberation socialist Malcolm X blamed King's pacifist approach to a cruel and unjust reality and the "white" liberal concept of reconciliation itself (Cone, *Martin & Malcolm & America*, 96–99). As will be discussed later, Cone's criticism of King, though not identi-cal to Malcolm X's, takes a similar stance, that King's seemingly passive "turn-the-other-cheek" method of reconciliation against a vicious racist system did not adequately serve the function of true liberation. Despite those criticisms, however, King's ideal of reconciliation stood firm, because King never forgot that without liberation of the oppressed, there can never be authentic recon-ciliation between the oppressors and the oppressed. In other words, reconcili-ation necessitates liberation.

end of King's civil rights movement, beyond the triumph of the op-pressed over the oppressors, was to effect this reconciliation. This is why King preaches, "God grant that we will be participants in this newness and this magnificent development. If we will but do it, we will bring about a new day of justice and brotherhood and peace. And that day the morning stars will sing together and the sons of God will shout for joy. God bless you."[30] As we will discuss later, this idea of reconciliation is one of the prominent themes in King's theological and political rhetoric. Noel Erskine observes that this reconciliatory idea is the major difference between King and Cone. While Erskine contends that King sees reconciliation as the ultimate goal of the black struggle, Cone's ultimate goal is liberation.[31]

Throughout his public preaching life, King was in close con-nection with the black theology that emerged in the 1950s.[32] In

---

30. Carson and Holloran, *A Knock*, 224.

31. Erskine, *King among the Theologians*, 127. Indeed, Cone is not satisfied with King's "white Jesus" nonviolence agenda. According to Cone, King's Jesus seems to tell blacks that "the only way to win political freedom is through nonviolence," and that Jesus "chose him because King was the least of the evils available." Thus, Cone believes, even though King's life and legacy has been a tremendous foundation for the development of black liberation theology, King's ideal method of reconciliation would not achieve true liberation. Cone eventually wants to establish an uncontaminated pure black theology of a black God revealed through the unique black experience as the real ground of black liberation (Cone, *Black Theology of Liberation*). Cone's criticism is, however, difficult to swallow, because in his black liberation theological agenda there is an inescapable (and also inappropriate) binary structure of "pure white theol-ogy" and "pure black theology." There is no real evidence, neither historically nor theologically, that either thing truly exists.

32. Cone argues that black theology's origin dates back to early 19th century, wherein activists like Richard Allen, Henry Highland Garnet, Nat Turner, Henry McNeal Turner fought to liberate the black people (Cone, *For My People*, 7). However, Howard Thurman, whose *Jesus and the Disinherited* King is said to have carried with him to the day he died, must have been the strongest influence on the formulation of King's own black theology. Thur-man argues that 1) Jesus himself was one of the downtrodden who actively resisted an unjust, dominant society with nonviolence; 2) God is on the side of the oppressed; and 3) forgiveness, love, and reconciliation are the final destiny both for the downcast and the privileged. We will see later how King creatively

light of that connection, we observe two of black theology's important contributions to King's theology: first, the idea of black liberation, and second, the ultimate reconciliation between the oppressed and their oppressors. Though other influences such as theological liberalism and personalism (which we will discuss later) may have further developed these ideas, it seems more likely that black theology was the core foundation of King's personal homiletic philosophy.

## At Morehouse

Morehouse College was the first academic institution that King attended. There, Benjamin E. Mays, the president of the college at that time, played a significant role in King's education. Mays served as King's mentor during his years at Morehouse, sharing his own teachings and philosophies that King later adopted and adapted to coin his own theology. He influenced King's theology and preaching on at least three subjects: humanity, American society, and God.

To the first point, Mays believed in and advocated for the dignity of all human beings. He once wrote, "[T]he dignity of each individual wherever he resides on the earth is tied up with the destiny of all men that inhabit the globe. Whether we like it or not, we cannot do anything about it."[33] Mays taught his students that no individual was the spiritual or intellectual inferior of another, regardless of race. In this respect, Lischer's assessment of Mays is quite right when he says, "Mays was a liberal who believed that human largesse would eventually overcome ignorance and prejudice and usher in a new era of understanding."[34] Indeed, we can easily discern Mays's conception of human dignity in King's later sermons, such as when he preaches, "The whole concept of the *imago dei*, as it is expressed in Latin, the 'image of God,' is the idea that all

---

adopts and adapts these key ideas of Thurman's for his own homiletic and theological usage.

33. Mays, *Disturbed About Man*, 22.

34. Lischer, *Preacher King*, 44.

men have something within them that God injected. . . . And this gives him a uniqueness, it gives him worth, it gives him dignity."[35]

Second, Mays thought that American democratic ideals did not match American society. According to Mays, if America had truthfully and faithfully followed the democratic ideals upon which it was founded, its society would have not become oppressive and bifurcated. This corruption of America was particularly clear from a Christian perspective. Mays writes:

> It is clear that Christian light condemns the inhumanity of man in our economic life. It is equally clear that Christian light condemns the corruption in our political life. We know what Christianity has to say about war and racial discrimination . . . What then can we do to be saved? It is the responsibility of the church of Christ to launch an evangelic campaign to convert men to God.[36]

Agreeing with Mays's Christian criticism of American society, King voiced a similar critique years later:

> On the one hand we have proudly professed the great principles of democracy, but on the other hand we have sadly practiced the very opposite of those principles. But now more than ever before, America is challenged to realize its dream, for the shape of the world today does not permit our nation the luxury of an anemic democracy. And the price that America must pay for the continued oppression of the Negro and other minority groups is the price of its own destruction. For the hour is late. And the clock of destiny is ticking out. We must act now before it is too late.[37]

In these statements, both Mays and King agree that American society has been corrupted by deviating from its original democratic dreams and must now be reformed and converted in the way God wants.

---

35. Carson and Holloran, *A Knock*, 88.

36. Mays, *Disturbed*, 22, 24.

37. Carson and Holloran, *A Knock*, 87.

Therefore, concerning theological notions of God, we find that Mays and King share another thought—in particular, what God wants us to do when we confront a dehumanized society. Mays says, "We need the power of God unto salvation . . . Ask God, and mean it, to create a clean heart and renew a right spirit within us. Ask him to purge our souls of sin and corruption."[38] Here Mays claims that God is fighting against the widespread injustice throughout America and that Christians are the people who had to carry out God's divine purpose. Simply put, God is with us in our fight against injustice. In King's later preaching, we see the same motif of God's presence with us in the fight against injustice. More specifically, King's preaching portrays a powerful and loving God that has begun the fight in his own name and calls upon us to join him. Indeed, for King this is the only true source of strength we have in the fight against injustice. He preaches, "It will give us courage to face the uncertainty of the future. It will give our tired feet new strength as we continue our forward stride toward the city of freedom."[39]

We realize that Mays's theological ideas concerning humanity, society, and God became the key themes that King would carry with him throughout his involvement in the civil rights movement. Of course, King did not take Mays's ideas whole cloth without developing them in his own ways. He rather adapted what he learned from his beloved teacher. For instance, King stressed how abundant God's love is for the oppressor, even when God is fighting on the side of the oppressed. Even the oppressors "are not totally bad and . . . are not beyond God's redemptive love."[40]

The three concerns that King learned from Mays at Morehouse were the same concerns he brought to Crozer Seminary and then to Boston University. At these two institutions, King would hone and develop what he had learned from Ebenezer and Morehouse to find his own theological voice.

38. Mays, *Disturbed*, 24.

39. King, *Strength to Love*, 114.

40. King, *Strength to Love*, 51.

## At Crozer Seminary

It was while attending Cozer Seminary that King was introduced to Christian liberalism, primarily through his favorite teacher, George Washington Davis. Under Davis's influence, King discovered the unity of all truth, universal principles acceptable to all people of goodwill, and the wholeness of both his secular world and religion.[41] King writes, "In fact the two cannot be separated; religion for me is life."[42] Of course, the fact that King was attracted to liberal theology and wrote some papers in favor of it does not mean that he abandoned his traditional theological notions. Rather, King gave up the whole liberal project years later.[43] Thus, we can only say that King was absorbing some fundamentals of liberalism, which he then subjected to his own alterations. For instance, he adopted "such Christian values as love and personality for their alleged conformity to the laws of the universe"[44] and appropriated them for his own preaching. King preached in his sermon *Loving your Enemies* the following:

> Far from being the pious injunction of a Utopian dreamer, the command to love one's enemy is an absolute necessity for our survival. Love even for enemies is the key

41. Lischer, *Preacher King*, 55. Davis argues that universal principles, such as love, justice, freedom, equality, peace, etc., undergird the fundamental structure of the world and must be sought by humanity out of goodwill for a better world. Obviously, these principles or principal ideas made their way into King's later theological and humanitarian ideas of love even for enemies, freedom of all races, social equality, and the absence of unjust war (Davis, "The Ethical Basis of Christian Theology," 177–89).

42. Lischer, *Preacher King*, 55.

43. Lischer, *Preacher King*, 59. In particular, King's theological mind cannot accept the liberal idea of Jesus not as God Incarnate but as "the best thinking about God the world has known to date" or the idea that there is no historical intervention by the Divine. However, as discussed above, even though he gave up the liberal project entirely, the remains of it still lingered in his mind and were expressed through his own alterations of its ideas.

44. Lischer, *Preacher King*, 55.

to the solution of the problems of our world. Jesus is not
an impractical idealist: he is the practical realist.[45]

It is evident in this sermon that King's notion of Christian love is very similar to liberalism's idea of love and its practical implications. What is then important for the sake of this research is the fact that King was absorbing liberalism's views of universality. Indeed, through these views, Christian liberalism was eagerly relating God to the secular world, not merely confining God to the religious realm. Where there is genuine love among people, there is also God—who is love itself. In King's preaching, this universality of God's nature is very important in his effort to have God speak to the secular realm directly through earthly witnesses, which was the very aim of the civil rights movement. Thus, King preaches, "in the universe there is a God of power who is able to do exceedingly abundant things in nature and in history."[46]

In short, we find the liberal influence on King in his later sermons, especially the idea of God's universal nature. This liberal influence started at Crozer Seminary through its academic environment. However, it was not until King arrived at Boston University that he was fully able to study Christian liberalism and, in particular, Boston personalism.

### At Boston University

Boston personalism had a huge impact on King, even though it would not be the ultimate theological ground of his civil rights movement. In a 1959 sermon, King says, "You look at me, Martin Luther King; you see my body, but, you must understand, my body can't think, my body can't reason. You don't see the 'me' that makes me me. You can never see my personality."[47] The personalism taught by Harold DeWolf and others at Boston University had a considerable influence on King's theology in two ways—its

45. King, *Strength to Love*, 49–50.

46. King, *Strength to Love*, 107.

47. King, *The Measure of a Man*, 51.

theism and Christology. Personalism espouses a God of ideal personality.[48] This God comes to a person in the form of a personal spirit and confronts that person in a religious experience.[49] And since it is in God's very nature to be personal, God is immanent in this world wherein the religious experience happens. However, it is not right to say that King accepted the immanence of God in the world by denying the transcendence of God. During his academic life at Crozer, King had already written, "Frankly I feel that unless God were transcendent he would not be God at all."[50] Throughout King's ministerial and public life, the ideas of the transcendence and immanence of God coexisted in King's theology.

What raises particular interest concerning King's exposure to Boston personalism is that King became acquainted with a God who reveals Godself to common persons in the world through God's personal spirit. As discussed already, for King, this idea of God does not mean that God does not have spiritual supremacy in relation to the world. Rather, this only means that King highly cherishes the concept of a personal God who has been revealing and confronting common persons or the public in the form of God's personal spirit all along. Thus, King wrote, "The revelation of God in Christ is not dissimilar to the revelation of God in other men [sic] but in Christ the revelation of God reaches its peak."[51] In other words, God still appears supreme in the special or ultimate revelation through Christ, but is also *personal enough* to have intimate relations with and be revealed through individual human beings.

At Boston, King was taught that "Jesus does not incarnate God in the orthodox Christian sense but represents the best thinking

48. For a more detailed personalist discussion of theology, see Knudson, *The Philosophy of Personalism*; Bowne, *Personalism*; Brightman, *Moral Laws*; DeWolf, *Theology of the Living Church*; and Muelder, *Moral Law in Christian Social Ethics*.

49. Concerning this notion of God, in an examination at Crozer King wrote, "God for me along with other theists is a personal spirit immanent in nature and in the value structure of the universe" (King, *Papers*, 290).

50. King, *Papers*, 291.

51. Lischer, *Preacher King*, 58.

about God the world has known to date."[52] Jesus was conceived as an amazing spiritual socialist as well as a religious revolutionary. Of course, we cannot think that King fully accepted this personalistic idea of Jesus, even though his notes from that time say, "It was the warmness of his devotion to God and the intimacy of his trust in God that accounted for his divinity."[53] For King, Jesus was still the spiritual and physical manifestation of God's presence in this world. Nonetheless, it was at least personalism's contribution to King that allowed him to find in every oppressed person the divinity and intellectual foundation that pertains to the human Jesus Christ. He once wrote:

> I studied philosophy and theology at Boston University under Edgar S. Brightman and L. Harold DeWolf. Both men greatly stimulated my thinking. It was mainly under these teachers that I studied personalistic philosophy—the theory that the clue to the meaning of ultimate reality is found in personality. The personal idealism remains today my basic philosophical position. Personalism's insistence that only personality—finite and infinite—is ultimately real strengthened me in two convictions; it gave me metaphysical and philosophical grounding for the idea of a personal God, and it gave me a metaphysical basis for the dignity and worth of all human personality.[54]

Evidently, this discovery of human divinity in every person was both challenging and inspirational for King. Later on it was logical that the personalist concept became an imperative of King's ministerial approach to the cruel reality of his day—namely, seeing goodness still inherent deep inside both the oppressed and the oppressors.

No doubt, personalism left a strong imprint in King's thought. However, as suggested before, King did not fully accept the personalist approach to theology, and therefore his years at Boston did not totally change King's traditional belief in church and God;

52. Lischer, *Preacher King*, 59.

53. Lischer, *Preacher King*.

54. King, *Stride toward Freedom*, 73.

rather, they equipped King with some critical liberal and socialist tools. Thus armed, King graduated from Boston University and arrived at Montgomery, Alabama, to start his ministerial and public life.

## Influences of Paul Tillich and Karl Barth

It is no surprise that King's theology was influenced by Paul Tillich, as King finished his dissertation on Tillich's theology in 1955. The year itself carried particular significance for King's own theology, since he was just starting his public life as a civil rights activist in Montgomery. Under the dissertation title, "A Comparison of the Conceptions of God in the Thinking of Paul Tillich and Henry Nelson Wieman," King explored Tillich's conception of God, some of which King took later for his own use. However, he maintained some distance from Tillich, as Tillich's God was too impersonal[55] to satisfy King's own homiletic theology, which, as demonstrated in the previous section, had been influenced by Boston personalism.

Nonetheless, Tillich's major influence on King comes from his conception of God. In Tillich's theology, God is perceived as the fundamental Ground of Being, Being itself, or the Power of Being.[56] Specifically this means that "God is the ground of the personal existence and participates in every life as its ground and aim."[57] This conception of God is essentially universal; God sustains, empowers, and directs everything that has being in the whole universe. In other words, God is the universal ground of any being. In this theological sense, for Tillich, "*The Word of God* means the self-manifestation of that which concerns everyone ultimately."[58]

---

55. Erskine, *King among the Theologians*, 47.

56. Paul Tillich, *The Shaking of the Foundations*; Paul Tillich, *The Courage to Be*, 7

57. Erskine, *King among the Theologians*, 25.

58. Erskine, *King among the Theologians*, 39.

In fact, we find Tillich's conception of God as the universal Ground of Being or the Power of Being in King's various sermons. In the sermon *Our God is Able,* King preaches:

> At the center of the Christian faith is the conviction that in the universe there is a God of power who is able to do exceedingly abundant things in nature and in history . . . Let us notice, first, that God is able to sustain the vast scope of the physical universe.[59]

And in the sermon *Paul's Letter to American Christians*:

> It is a telescope through which we look out into the long vista of eternity and the love of God breaking forth into time. It is an eternal reminder to a power-drunk generation that love is [the] most durable power in the world, and that it is at bottom the heartbeat of the moral cosmos. Only through achieving this love can you expect to matriculate into the university of eternal life.[60]

Finally, in his sermon *Guidelines for a Constructive Church*:

> The acceptable year of the Lord is that year when men learn to live together as brothers. The acceptable year of the Lord is that year when men will keep their theology abreast with their technology . . . The acceptable year of the Lord is that year when men will beat their swords into plowshares, and their spears into pruning hooks; and nations will not rise up against nations, neither will they study war anymore. The acceptable year of the Lord is that year when every valley shall be exalted, and every mountain will be made low; the rough places would be made plain, and the crooked places straight; and the glory of the Lord shall be revealed, and all flesh shall see it together.[61]

Thus, King preaches that God is a universal God who sustains, empowers, illuminates, and embraces the whole universe. Of course,

---

59. King, *Strength to Love,* 107.

60. Carson and Holloran, *A Knock,* 36.

61. Carson and Holloran, *A Knock,* 112–13.

we might argue that this perception of God could just as easily have come from such sources as King's own black church tradition and, to some extent, that argument is true. However, King owes, at the very least, the language of this universal God to Tillich.

Tillich's idea of God played a significant role in King's public life from 1955 on. King's God had to be universal enough to embrace the whole American socio-political and cultural reality. Nonetheless, as Erskine points out above, King could not fully accept Tillich's perception of God, since Tillich's God was too impersonal[62] for King to develop his own pastoral and prophetic voice. King's proclaimed God, who is the eternal Ground of the whole Universe, had to be personal in order to have a compassionate relation with other beings, just as he preaches:

> Man, for Jesus, is not mere flotsam and jetsam in the river of life, but a child of God. Is it not unreasonable to assume that God, whose creative activity is expressed in an awareness of a sparrow's fall and the number of hairs on a man's head, excludes from his encompassing love the life of man itself?[63]

As discussed before, this personal characteristic of the universal God was provided to King through the personalist discipline at Boston. At this point, therefore, we can conclude that King was forming his own homiletic theology by synthesizing personalism and Tillich's theology, among other elements.

While Tillich's influence on King is explicit, Barth's influence seems less so. In some cases, such as his sermon "Pilgrimage to Non-violence," King criticizes Barth's neo-orthodoxy. King says, "In its revolt against overemphasis on the power of reason in liberalism, neo-orthodoxy fell into a mood of antirationalism and semifundamentalism, stressing a narrow uncritical Biblicism. This approach, I felt, was inadequate both for the church and for personal life."[64] Still, it is incorrect to say that Barth's theology does not have any connection to King's. King himself wrote in his Boston

---

62. Erskine, *King among the Theologians*, 47.

63. King, *Strength to Love*, 124.

64. King, *Strength to Love*, 147.

graduation paper, "In spite of our somewhat severe criticism of Barth, however, we do not in the least want to minimize the importance of his message."[65] In fact, Barth and King share at least two similar ideas.

First, both of them agree that the human situation itself is so desperate and corrupt that Christians should evaluate it and take action. Barth once said:

> I have now become a member of the Social Democratic Party. Just because I set such emphasis Sunday by Sunday upon the last things, it was no longer possible for me personally to remain suspended in the clouds above the present evil world but rather it had to be demonstrated here and now that faith in the Greatest does not exclude but rather includes within it work and suffering in the realm of the imperfect.[66]

Although Barth's theology seems to begin with the other-worldly God, his theology is rooted in facing human desperation here and now. This is why King states, "[Barth's] cry does call attention to the desperateness of the human situation."[67] King also recognized this "desperateness" and went radically beyond Barth's position with his own actions and preaching. King was bold enough to take a public stance on a national level and encouraged the oppressed to take their own action toward social transformation, as he preached, "With this faith we will be able to hew out of the mountain of despair the stone of hope. With this faith we will be able to transform the jangling discords of our nation into a beautiful symphony of brotherhood."[68] For King, the real action from the oppressed was urgent for true transformation to come.

Second, both Barth and King had no qualms in proclaiming God's universal dominion over the present as the only right answer to the human condition. King continues his comments on Barth's theology as follows:

65. King, *Papers*, vol. 2, 106.
66. Barth, *Revolutionary Theology*, 28.
67. King, *Papers*, vol. 2, 106.
68. Carson and Holloran, *A Knock*, 224.

[Barth] does insist that religion begins with God and that man cannot have faith apart from him. He does proclaim that apart from God our human efforts turn to ashes and our sunrises into darkest night. He does suggest that man is not sufficient unto himself for life, but is dependent upon the proclamation of God's living Word, through which by means of Bible, preacher, and revealed Word, God himself comes to the consciences of men.[69]

Barth recognizes God's dominion in the present moment as a transforming power in the world. For Barth, this God is the only effective answer to human decadence. As Jesus comes to this world in flesh (John, 1:14), God's real dominion over evil descends with him. It is no wonder that King's actions and message stood on common ground with Barth. For King, it is the same God that both overcomes the evil of the world and is the only true resource upon which we may rely "to win our freedom."[70] Thus, King had no doubt that "[t]he judgment of God is upon us today."[71]

It is interesting that King had considerable exposure to the theologies of both Tillich and Barth when he was crafting his homiletic voice. He certainly knew that each theologian had his own strengths to emulate and weaknesses to avoid. As a result, by the time King began his work as a Christian pastor, he was utilizing these strengths to speak out in his own unique voice.

## King amidst a Violent Reality

Just as the black church strongly influenced King, the sociopolitical, economic, and spiritual environment of his time also shaped his theology and public life. In particular, the violence with which he found himself surrounded led to King's homiletic idea of God manifested through(out) the whole universe.[72] This

69. King, *Papers*, vol. 2, 106.

70. Carson and Holloran, *A Knock*, 223.

71. Carson and Holloran, *A Knock*, 220.

72. Of course, it might not be entirely correct to say here that the context of violence was the sole or even primary cause of King's idea of God spoken

theological development was natural for King for two reasons. Firstly, twofold violence (social and spiritual) appeared to be universal—that is, violence existed everywhere there was an imbalance of privilege—and the universal God is the counterclaimant against universe-permeating violence. Secondly, this God of the whole universe is biased toward neither the oppressed nor the oppressor. God does not desire an ultimate triumphant victory of the oppressed over the oppressors, but rather seeks reconciliation between the two opposing parties. The victory of one side is simply a pathway to that ultimate purpose.[73] Below is a discussion on this critical issue of violence and the God of the universe in societal, physical, spiritual, and moral senses.

### Societal and Physical Violence

We can quickly discuss the societal and physical violence of King's time in two ways: at the international level and the domestic—or societal—level. From the 1940s through the 1960s, America was involved in several global wars, namely World War II, the Korean War, and the Vietnam War. These wars created national instability due to monetary shortage, numerous casualties, collective anxiety for the future, economic uncertainty, and so forth. The Vietnam War in particular was a huge failure for America and that failure sparked severe criticism from both inside and outside the U.S.

---

through the whole universe. As demonstrated in earlier chapters, King's theological struggles and interactions with his own historical context over almost a decade led him to that particular notion of God. Indeed, the seed of King's homiletic idea of God spoken through the whole universe was planted even earlier, in his childhood at Ebenezer.

73. Smith and Zepp, in their *Search for the Beloved Community* (141–45), recognize both the Jewish conception of the messianic era and the early Christian proclamation and doctrine of the Kingdom of God as the foundational ground for King's dream of the Beloved Community, the community where all conflicting parties eventually come to live in peace and harmony. They also notice that in order to achieve this wondrous dream, King's God should be the God of the universe, who continuously comes to humanity as ever-loving and ever-proclaimed. We will explore this issue of the Beloved Community and the God of the universe in more detail later, when we deal with King's eschatology.

King was among these outspoken critics. Preaching at Ebenezer Baptist on the topic, he stated:

> They see the children selling their sisters to our soldiers, soliciting for their mothers. We [Americans] have destroyed their two most cherished institutions—the family and the village. We have destroyed their land and their crops . . . We have corrupted their women and children and killed their men. What strange liberators we are![74]

King did not at first vocally oppose the war, but by 1963, having already long embraced the ideals of pacifism (influenced in particular by Gandhi), King expressed deep concerns regarding the conflict in Vietnam. He did so because, among other reasons, he believed that it is inconsistent to preach against violence at home but to keep silent against the country's international crime.[75]

More importantly King believed that America, on the domestic level, was an explicit example of a violent society that oppressed the marginalized within its own borders, especially black people. From childhood, though he grew up in "a home of economic security and relative comfort,"[76] King recognized the social and economic problems afflicting black people. He recalls:

> I had grown up abhorring not only segregation but also the oppressive and barbarous acts that grew out of it. I had passed spots where Negroes had been savagely lynched, and had watched the Ku Klux Klan on its rides

74. Lischer, *Preacher King*, 161.

75. Other reasons include that the message against the war would help his allegiance with black youths in the ghetto whose antiwar ethos was already strong as well as his connection with white liberals whose focus was moving from the civil rights movement to the peace movement and that the unjust causes and immorality championed by the war were almost identical to the injustice and immorality the civil rights movement fought against. Thus, taking a stance against the Vietnam war was itself taking a stand against the injustice that oppressed black people at home. Above all, however, as he confirmed through his preaching against the war, his primary reason was his Christian moral conscience, which could not ignore the causes and effects of such a war—inhuman cruelty, human arrogance, and the exploitation of the underprivileged (Ansboro, *Martin Luther King, Jr.*, 256–65).

76. King, *Stride toward Freedom*, 90.

at night. I had seen police brutality with my own eyes, and watched Negroes receive the most tragic injustice in the courts . . . So when I went to Atlanta's Morehouse College as a freshman in 1944 my concern for racial and economic justice was already substantial.[77]

Therefore, it comes as no surprise that during his days at Morehouse King read *Thoreau's Essay on Civil Disobedience* several times, a book that introduced the idea of nonviolent resistance into King's consciousness.[78]

When King arrived in Montgomery, Alabama, for his first pastorate position, he witnessed the continuing severity of black people's oppression. He recounted the poverty and oppression of the black people in Montgomery thus:

> 63 percent of the Negro women workers in Montgomery are domestics, and 48 percent of the Negro men are laborers or domestic workers . . . in 1950 the median income for the approximately 70,000 white people of Montgomery was $1730, compared with $970 for the 50,000 Negroes. Ninety-four percent of the white families in Montgomery have flush toilets inside their homes, while only 31 percent of the Negro families enjoy such facilities.[79]

Beyond these socio-economical infrastructure problems, what most troubled King's mind was the apparent denial of basic (God-given) human rights to his black friends, colleagues, congregants, and neighbors. This situation was exponentially escalating the tension between blacks and whites.

On December 1st, 1955, an incident took place that would serve as the launching point for King's public life. On that day, a woman named Rosa Parks, after a long day at work, refused to yield her bus seat to a white person. She was arrested, despite the fact that she was not actually in violation of any segregation law, since she was sitting in the first row of the black section at the

77. King, *Stride toward Freedom*, 90–91.

78. King, *Stride toward Freedom*, 91.

79. King, *Stride toward Freedom*, 27–28.

back of the bus. However, because the bus was full, the bus driver demanded that Parks give up her seat to allow a white man to sit. This incident triggered an outraged response from the black community in Montgomery and led to King's election as the president of the Montgomery Improvement Association and spokesperson for Rosa Parks. King was officially in the public eye and would remain there until his death, fighting vocally for the liberation of his people.[80]

According to King himself, his method of nonviolent resistance was rooted in the philosophies of two great thinkers: Mohandas K. Gandhi and the social philosopher Walter Rauschenbusch. King was first attracted to Gandhi's concept of *satyagraha*, which means truth-force or love-force. Intrigued by the power that lies in the marriage of the concepts of love and force, he writes, "Gandhi was probably the first person in history to lift the love ethic of Jesus above mere interaction between individuals to a powerful and effective social force on a large scale."[81] Therefore, it was natural that King, from the very beginning of his Montgomery movement, engaged exclusively in nonviolent resistance against his aggressive opponents. He continuously urged the members of his movement to work within the confines of the law, not to use any physical force—rather to suffer before using violence. This is why Rosa Parks was an ideal symbol of the civil rights movement. As King says:

> Mrs. Rosa Parks is a fine person. And since it had to happen, I am happy it happened to a person like Mrs. Parks, for nobody can doubt the boundless outreach of her integrity. Nobody can doubt the height of her character, nobody can doubt of her Christian commitment and devotion to the teaching of Jesus.[82]

---

80. For more biographical information on King, refer to Lewis, *King: A Critical Biography*; Lischer, *Preacher King*; and Martin Luther King, *Stride toward Freedom*. King's own book, of course, is the best testament to King's personal philosophies regarding the Montgomery movement.

81. King, *Stride toward Freedom*, 97.

82. Lischer, *Preacher King*, 86.

As seen above, King considered moral integrity, quality of character, and adherence to Jesus's teachings of nonviolence as the key components of social action, making it easy to reconcile these notions of nonviolent resistance to Gandhi's *satyagraha*.

Walter Rauschenbusch's book *Christianity and the Social Crisis* also had a considerable influence on King. Even though King believed Rauschenbusch's thought to be flawed in some respects—such as (1) a superficial optimism concerning man's nature, and (2) identification of the Kingdom of God with a particular social and economic system[83]—he admitted that Rauschenbusch's work was the theological basis for his social concerns.[84] What King inherited from Rauschenbusch was the idea that the gospel should deal with *the whole person*. Christianity—or any religion, for that matter—should be concerned not only with the soul, but with the body as well. This means that the gospel must also be concerned with social and economic conditions that damage the soul. If the gospel concerns only the spirit, it is not a whole gospel and does not contain the whole truth.

King was attracted to Rauschenbusch's ideas because he needed a religion that addressed both the concrete human situation and worldly affairs. Accordingly, King eagerly sought and proclaimed a God who actively participated in human life in order to transform a violent reality and liberate the oppressed. King's God could not be blind to the voices of the oppressed and exist in the religious realm alone. God must be a God of world-transformation.

## Spiritual and Moral Violence

The brutal societal and physical violence against black people was, of course, the driving force behind King's public works and the formation of his homiletic theology. However, there was also a secondary kind of violence against which King fought—a violence of the spiritual and moral kind. Throughout his public life, King openly criticized this spiritual and moral violence that pertained to

83. King, *Stride toward Freedom*, 91.

84. King, *Stride toward Freedom*, 91.

the church and its leaders as well as political leadership. In King's "Letter From Birmingham City Jail," we see how this spiritual and moral violence had been hovering over King's public life and how that influenced King to create his own homiletic theology.

In the letter, King recounts that as soon as he started his public protest in Montgomery, he incurred backlash from church and societal leadership. King initially expected the support of the white churches in Montgomery. Instead, the city's white spiritual leaders, rather than being King's strongest allies, were often outright opponents, refusing to endorse the freedom movement and even misrepresenting the protest's leaders.[85] The moral decay of the legal system provoked further anger on the part of black protesters; most judges and juries were likely to ignore the law in favor of prejudice.

As King says in the letter, the situation in Birmingham was no better than that in Montgomery. There, King suffered threefold spiritual and moral deprivation. First, white clergy in the city criticized King, saying that his nonviolent activity was extreme.[86] Further, according to King, the clergy "warmly commended the Birmingham police force for 'keeping order' and 'preventing violence.'"[87] This opposition was experienced by King as spiritual and moral violence against the whole black community as well as himself. King firmly believed that the church was the first and last shelter and protector of the oppressed and marginalized and should therefore be the eager advocate of justice. However, King found the mindset of the white church depraved to the extent that he had to say:

> Over and over again I have found myself asking: "What kind of people worship here: Who is their God? . . . The contemporary church is often a weak, ineffectual voice with an uncertain sound. It is so often the arch-supporter of the status quo. Far from being disturbed by the presence of the church, the power structure of the average

85. Washington, *Testament of Hope*, 299.

86. Washington, *Testament of Hope*, 296.

87. Washington, *Testament of Hope*, 301.

community is consoled by the church's silent and often vocal sanction of things as they are."[88]

It would be seriously mistaken to say that all white churches and their pastors turned against King. There were some small exceptions. Some white pastors lost their pulpits and some white friends were murdered thanks to their sincerest sympathy to King and the civil rights movement. Yet still, it was depressing for King that the majority of the white church was not, he believed, on God's side.

Second, King was the victim of spiritual and moral violence from his own people, both middle-class blacks and those who belonged to various black nationalist groups—such as Elijah Muhammad's Muslim movement. Black people in the middle class were not only accustomed to and even comfortable in segregated society but were also indifferent to the civil rights movement, even criticizing it as social disorder. As King saw it, they "have been so completely drained of self-respect and a sense of 'somebodiness' that they have adjusted to segregation."[89] Black people involved in the black nationalist groups were responsible for another form of moral violence. Not only had they repudiated Christianity, but they also advocated violence as an effective tool for social change and labeled all white people the "devil."[90]

The third form of spiritual and moral violence came from the "white moderate"[91] and political leadership. King said, in the Birmingham City Jail letter and elsewhere, that the white moderate always told black people to "wait" for the right time; but the call for "wait" always meant "never." In the middle of the letter, King included a portion of another letter from a white brother in Texas that read, "All Christians know that the colored people will receive equal rights eventually, but it is possible that you are in too great of a religious hurry. It has taken Christianity almost two thousand years to accomplish what it has. The teachings of Christ take time

88. Washington, *Testament of Hope*, 299–300.
89. Washington, *Testament of Hope*, 296.
90. Washington, *Testament of Hope*, 296–97.
91. Washington, *Testament of Hope*, 296.

to come to earth."[92] For King, what was clear in this letter was that the white moderates wanted to maintain the status quo from a distorted perspective of Christianity. That sort of "Christianized" attitude to the civil rights movement could not have been more violent, in King's opinion. It was a spiritually and morally violent act committed in the name of Christianity. King received a similar response from socio-political leaders in Birmingham. Even though they were probably religious people of Christian faith, "the city fathers" of Birmingham "consistently refused to engage in good faith negotiation" to improve the life situations of black people.[93]

What King experienced as spiritual and moral violence, and revealed in his letter, was not a phenomenon unique to Birmingham. As he said, the situation had been the same since his first public protest in Montgomery and, as we know now, it would continue up to and even beyond his assassination. Amazingly enough, King did not retreat from his stance. Rather, he pronounced the abundance of God's universal justice, peace, and love among all people, despite their spiritual and moral violence. King believed that God was unchangeably on the side of justice and love, which would ultimately suffuse the nation. He proclaims in the closing of his letter:

> One day the South will know that when these disinherited children of God sat down at lunch counters they were in reality standing up for the best in the American dream and the most sacred values in our Judeo-Christian heritage, and thusly, carrying our whole nation back to those great walls of democracy which were dug deep by the Founding Fathers in the formulation of the Constitution and the Declaration of Independence.[94]

Here we begin to glimpse that King's profound theology of reconciliation defies the death-sting of violence and bridges the extreme chasm permeating the whole of American society. For King this national or universal reconciliation is no longer a "dream," but

92. Washington, *Testament of Hope*, 296.

93. Washington, *Testament of Hope*, 290.

94. Washington, *Testament of Hope*, 302.

a reality promised in the Judeo-Christin heritage and engraved in the nation's Constitution. God has started the work of reconciliation already, and we are invited to participate in it as God's partners.

## Summary

What is clear from what we have discussed thus far is that King's preaching theology developed over time, drawing on a variety of experiential and intellectual sources—from his childhood at Ebenezer to academic influences to actual public ministry. Indeed, most of the quotations used in this chapter come from the writing, preaching, and public speaking that followed King's graduation from Boston in 1955, when the basic formulation of his homiletic theology was complete. Therefore, we can summarize his homiletic theological development as follows. King initially formulated his theology along black, Baptist, evangelical, and fundamentalist lines, eventually departing from these toward the confrontation of and struggle with theological liberalism (specifically, personalism in Boston). Later on, by adoption and synchronization of all those various sources of experience and theology, he came to create his own concrete theological ideas.

Of course, this is not to say that King's homiletic theology and sermonic philosophy stopped their development after his graduation from academia (as we will see later, for instance, King's moral attitude vis-à-vis the Vietnam War changes over time), but only that he completed his basic synthetic theological formulation before embarking upon his public ministry. These basic ideas include a personal God of the universe,[95] upon which he forges his fully fledged reconciliatory and ecumenical writings, sermons, and speeches. In fact, the cruel spiritual and social violence King faced, endured, and finally overcame in the public arena was the very occasion for the development of a complete homiletic theology of

95. This is King's creative synthesis of the fundamentalist notion of an omnipotent and omnipresent God and the Boston personalist understanding of God.

the personal God of the universe. The next chapter begins with a detailed discussion of this particular idea of the universal God and other associated theological concepts as best demonstrated in his preaching.

# 2

# King's God Manifested through the Universe and Violent Reality

KING ONCE PREACHED, "[I]N the universe there is a God of power who is able to do exceedingly abundant things in nature and in history."[1] This proclamation demonstrates his reconciliatory homiletic theology of God manifested through(out) the universe; that is, God represents Godself in the world by being manifested (or proclaimed) throughout the universe, and humanity—more specifically, the preacher—reinterprets this God of the universe through her/his proclamation, aided by the Word.

As seen in the discussion up to this point, King, via the relationship between his religious and intellectual resources, formed this homiletic theological thought and adroitly integrated that idea into his reconciliatory preaching and speeches. Who then, exactly, is this God for King, and what is this God able to do in the universe? Additionally, what characteristics does this God have? Who is then Jesus in relation to this God? And finally, how are we human beings to live in God's universe? In King's sermons and important speeches we find the answers to these questions in his own words.

1. King, *Strength to Love*, 107.

# God, Humanity, Jesus, and the Universe and Evil

## God

Above all else, King preaches God as revealed through the whole universe. For King, God is the whole truth and the universal law manifested to all common people. He preaches:

> At the center of the Christian faith is the conviction that in the universe there is a God of power who is able to do exceedingly abundant things in nature and in history. This conviction is stressed over and over in the Old and the New Testaments. Theologically, this affirmation is expressed in the doctrine of the omnipotence of God . . . When our days become darker than a thousand midnights, let us remember that there is a great benign Power in the universe whose name is God, and he is able to make a way out of no way, and transform dark yesterdays into bright tomorrows.[2]

In these words, we find two of King's most significant homiletic emphases. The first of these is that God has already been proclaimed through the whole of nature and human history (i.e., the whole cosmos). The Old and New Testaments are the two main places where this cosmic God is explicitly manifested. Hence, in relation to this God, what human beings have to do is simply to *remember*[3] the God who is already known to us. Besides, since God has been proclaimed to us from the beginning of the universe, the preacher's first role is not to search for or even rediscover God—as if God were not known—but to re-represent God's self-manifestation through speech rooted in the Word.

Secondly, this manifestation of God as the whole truth and the universal law is significant for King because God, through the act of self-proclamation, takes the initiative in love to transform a violent reality to a reconciled one. In other words, the God in King's homiletic theology is a God who manifests Godself as the

2. King, *Strength to Love*, 107, 114.

3. King, *Strength to Love*, 107–14. Throughout his sermon, "Our God Is Able," King often uses the word, "notice."

universal law and tears down the violent forces in the world by that law in love, thus creating a new reality. Having this homiletic theology in mind, King writes, "Whatever the name, some extra-human force labors to create a harmony out of the discords of the universe. There is a creative force that works to pull down mountains of evil and level hilltops of injustice. God still works through history his wonders to perform."[4] And again he preaches:

> In anxiety and hope, I read these words: "The United States Supreme Court today unanimously ruled bus segregation unconstitutional in Montgomery, Alabama." My heart throbbed with an inexpressible joy. The darkest hour of our struggle had become the first hour of victory. Someone shouted from the back of the courtroom, "God Almighty has spoken from Washington."[5]

Again, it is clear King's God is a universal and *historical* God of redemption and transformation. Alongside faithful human hands, God has been "busy" making positive changes in this world that definitely include the U.S. Supreme Court.

The last thing we should examine is King's notion of God as a personal God. God, as the universal power, the universal law, or the whole truth, is at the same time so personal that God communicates with his beloved human creations. This loving example leads people who listen to the Word to love even their enemies. King convincingly preaches:

> Now there is a final reason I think that Jesus says, "Love your enemies." It is this: that love has within it redemptive power. And there is a power there that eventually transforms individuals. That's why Jesus says, "Love your enemies." Because if you hate your enemies, you have no way to redeem and to transform your enemies. But, if you love your enemies, you will discover that at the very root of love is the power of redemption.[6]

4. King, *Stride toward Freedom*, 69–70.

5. Carson and Holloran, *A Knock*, 78.

6. Carson and Holloran, *A Knock*, 53.

For King, this love has the transformative power to affect redemption for one's enemies. In this sense, the transforming love within Christians cannot be limited to the individual. As God's love is universal, the Christian love that can conquer an enemy's hate is also universal, more specifically communal in its nature. King confirms that this Christian love originates from the revelation of a personal God.

In sum, in King's preaching, we meet the personal God who has already been proclaimed through the whole of nature and history, and this God, through self-proclamation, transforms violent reality. As discussed, this God is a personal and loving God who hates violence but nonetheless commands us to love our enemies. How, then, are humans to respond and react to this God? Do we fully accept the love of God towards humans or do we turn against God? Do we also hate the violence and encourage each other to love our enemies or do we often use the violence for the sake of various individual or societal desires? More theologically, who are we humans before God's eyes? In King's sermons, we find some answers to these questions.

## Humanity

King understands humanity in light of a key theological notion, namely, *the image of God*. King once wrote:

> Our Hebraic-Christian tradition refers to this inherent dignity of man [sic] in the Biblical term *the image of God*. This innate worth referred to in the phrase the image of God is universally shared in equal portions by all men. There is no graded scale of essential worth: there is no divine right of one race which differs from the divine right of another. Every human being has etched in this personality the indelible stamp of the creator.[7]

Here, we find two important understandings of humanity, which also color many of King's sermons. First, King contends that all

7. Washington, *Testament of Hope*, 118–19.

people, whether they are black or white, man or woman, healthy or disabled, rich or poor, etc., universally possess innate worth, because they reflect the image of God. Hence, all people deserve life, happiness, freedom, and respect. No one should be denied this universal divine right. In fact, this is the very ground upon which King urges his audience to, "Love your enemies."[8] King continuously insists that even human enemies can be loved and invited to participate in true "brotherhood."[9]

Second, because all people are inherently worthy, any form of violence must be denied and resisted. This is only because "every human being has etched in his personality the indelible stamp of the creator."[10] In this respect, any kind of violence against any person is a violation of that creator's stamp. Hence, for King, social and economic injustice, political inequity, segregation, racism, wars, etc.—not only in America but worldwide—must be resisted in God's name. In particular, black people, as an oppressed group in America, should recognize this divine right of living and resist the violence surrounding them.

Guided by these two key understandings of the human situation, King took direct action to resist violence around the nation, especially violence against black people. However, direct action does not mean violent action against individual oppressors or the oppressive society itself. Rather, King took nonviolent action, or direct action *in love,* against the oppressors. This is not because King believed violence was ineffective, or because he did not have the capacity for violence, but because he understood that even oppressors had innate worth as images of God. As King said:

> A vigorous enforcement of civil rights will bring an end
> to segregated public facilities which are barriers to a truly
> desegregated society, but it cannot bring an end to fears,
> prejudice, pride, and irrationality, which are the barriers
> to a truly integrated society. Those dark and demonic
> responses will be removed only as men are possessed

8. Carson and Holloran, *A Knock,* 53.

9. King, *Trumpet of Conscience,* 25.

10. Washington, *Testament of Hope,* 119.

by the invisible, inner law which etches on their hearts
the conviction that all men are brothers, and that love is
mankind's most potent weapon for personal and social
transformation.[11]

In this address, it is evident that King recognizes the innate human and divine worth of even his oppressors and hopes to share brotherhood with them.

Only direct resistance through love will touch the hearts of the oppressors and lead to the true transformation of society into a reality in which oppressor and oppressed are reconciled. How does one take such loving action? Is it even possible for humans to do so? King's answer to that question is simple: yes, through the manifestation of the personal God. God has already manifested Godself through nature and history by God's loving action towards all humans, regardless of if they are the oppressed or the oppressors. This is the only hope we have of taking direct resistant action in love.

Of course, we also need a tangible example to follow, since we are also weak in will and determination to take genuine direct action in love against this violent world. This is why Jesus is given to us as a gift to help us to carry out acts of sacrificial love in the name of God.

## Jesus

It is obvious that humans, whether Christian or not, find it difficult to embrace nonviolence, as such action requires—without exception—sacrifice made in love. In this situation, King knew, what people need is a real example of nonviolent sacrificial love carried out in the name of God. As this example, King holds up Jesus.

King describes Jesus as "the supreme manifestation of love."[12] In other words, Jesus is the most tangible manifestation of the personal loving God in the universe. In this regard, King preaches:

11. Washington, *Testament of Hope*, 124.
12. Erskine, *King among the Theologians*, 143.

> In our quest to make neighborly love a reality, we have, in addition to the inspiring example of the good Samaritan, the magnanimous life of our Christ to guide us. His altruism was universal, for he thought of all men [sic], even publicans and sinners, as brothers. His altruism was dangerous, for he willingly traveled hazardous roads in a cause he knew was right. His altruism was excessive, for he chose to die on Calvary, history's most magnificent expression of obedience to the unenforceable.[13]

Jesus's death on the cross and his resurrection are especially vivid symbols of Jesus's nonviolent action, through which violence is conquered. King further states, "The cross is the eternal expression of the length to which God will go in order to restore broken community. The resurrection is a symbol of God's triumph over all the forces that seek to block community."[14] In fact, this symbolic power leads King to the notion that "[t]he love of God manifested in the cross of Christ requires social justice as a basis for authentic community."[15] At this point, it seems clear that King's Jesus, who is the manifestation of the personal loving God of the universe, is also the Jesus who practices social justice and liberates his people from oppression and violence. King, indeed, always had this liberating Jesus in his mind and carried that Jesus wherever he went. So, James Cone couldn't be more right when he reflects on King's message and life as follows:

> As a prophet, with a Charisma never before witnessed in this century, King preached black liberation in the light of Jesus Christ and thus aroused the spirit of freedom among black people . . . his life and message demonstrate that the "soul" of the black community is inseparable from liberation, but always liberation grounded in Jesus Christ. The task of Black Theology is to build on the foundation laid by King by recognizing the theological character of the black community, a community where

13. King, *Strength to Love*, 38.

14. King, *Stride toward Freedom*, 105–6.

15. Erskine, *King among the Theologians*, 143.

being is inseparable from liberation through Jesus Christ.[16]

Cone nearly identifies King's life with that of Jesus by their shared ideas of freedom and liberation. Yet, he also seems to realize that King saw himself solely as a follower of Christ's example—the example that King hoped many other Christians, especially his own black people, would imitate as he strived to in humbleness.

In sum, King preaches that Jesus is the best manifestation of the universal God's sacrificial love, which boldly and directly resists a violent reality. King particularly emphasizes Jesus' universality in his nonviolent action in love. Since Jesus's love universally penetrates the world, there is a real hope that we can transform our violent reality into a reconciled one. In particular, it is Jesus's universal love that King utilized in his public life to resist violence, because King believed that the universal love of Jesus can not only transform an individual's life, but also the ways of an entire society. King, in Jesus and his life, finds the way by which all humanity share true brotherhood in one God.

In the next section, we turn to a discussion of how King perceives the universe where God, humanity, and Jesus work together to resist evil. Also, we will discuss what eschatological social status King pursues in his preaching against the unacceptable social evils of his age. Through this discussion, we will at last reach our central discussion: the essential roles of preaching, the preacher, and the pulpit in King's reconciliatory homiletic theology.

### The Universe, Evil, and Eschatology

Investigating how King perceives the universe in which God, humanity, and Jesus work together to resist a violent reality enables us to see the foundation upon which King's preaching is established. Walter Wink provides some insight in this endeavor. In his outstanding book *Engaging the Powers*, Wink articulates five basic worldviews (or five views of the universe) that people have.

16. Cone, *Black Theology of Liberation*, 77.

The first view is the ancient worldview. In this worldview, "everything earthly has its heavenly counterpart, and everything heavenly has its earthly counterpart."[17] For example, if a war happens on the earth between nations, then the same war happens in heaven between the angels of the nations. The Bible reflects this worldview in some places.

The second view is the spiritualistic or gnostic worldview. Wink observes, "What distinguishes this worldview from all other types is that it divides human beings into 'soul' and 'body'. . . in this account, the created order is evil, false and corrupted."[18] Thus, only that which pertains and belongs to the heavenly realm is true or desirable (because it is only in heaven that perfection exists). In contrast, the earthly realm is imperfect and evil. In this corrupt world, one's salvation "comes through knowledge of one's lost heavenly origins and the secret of the way back."[19] We also find this worldview in some places in the Bible and most of the gnostic writings.

The third view is the materialistic worldview. According to this worldview, there is no God, no soul, and no spiritual world. The spiritual world is an illusion. The world and human beings are merely complex amalgams of basic materials. Since the Enlightenment many Christians have espoused this worldview. Of course, in the Bible, we do not find this kind of worldview.

The fourth view is the theological worldview, which stands against materialism. This worldview adopted by most of theological liberalism and neo-orthodoxy separates the earthly and heavenly realms. While the heavenly realm cannot be known by the senses, the earthly realm is fully exposed (or, if not yet exposed, discoverable) to human knowledge through science.

The last worldview, which Wink advocates for, is an integral worldview. Wink describes this worldview as follows:

17. Wink, *Engaging the Powers*, 4.

18. Wink, *Engaging the Powers*, 4.

19. Wink, *Engaging the Powers*, 4.

> [This worldview] sees everything as having an outer and
> an inner aspect. It attempts to take seriously the spiritual
> insights of the ancient or biblical worldview by affirm-
> ing a withinness or interiority in all things, but sees this
> inner spiritual reality as inextricably related to an outer
> concretion or physical manifestation . . . It appears that
> everything, from photon to subatomic particles to corpo-
> rations to empires, has both an outer and inner aspect.[20]

In this respect, all earthly things, such as the political, economic,
and cultural institutions of our day, are integrated with heavenly
concerns. Wink concludes that we should acknowledge the evil
at the center of political, economic, and cultural institutions and
attempt to redeem the principalities and powers under the evil
scheme and centered at those institutions.[21]

King's preaching theology seems to strongly demonstrate
the "integral" worldview Wink provides above, in particular in
terms of (a) the mutual belonging of the inner spiritual reality and
outer physical manifestation, and (b) the evil centered within actual political, economic, and cultural institutions. Obviously, King
does not preach that the earthly realm has an exact counterpart
in heaven, that earthly life is false and worthless, or that the world
is strictly material and not spiritual, or that the heavenly realm is
totally separated from the earthly realm. Instead, King preaches
that spirituality, whether it is good or evil,[22] is at the very center
of people's everyday life.[23] Thus, King encourages us to redeem or

20. Wink, *Engaging the Powers*, 5.

21. Wink, *Engaging the Powers*, 5–10.

22. Throughout all King's sermons and speeches, the term "evil" refers to
socioeconomic and political evil or universal evil wearing socioeconomic and
political clothing. King does not try to explain the origin of this evil. Instead,
he only articulates how universal evil works and finally will be defeated in
human history. See King's *Strength to Love*.

23. In adopting this integral worldview, King both implicitly and explicitly
demonstrates what his theology inherits, especially from George Davis and
Paul Tillich. First, Davis's idea of wholeness of the secular world (material)
and religion (spiritual) almost identically reflects what the integral worldview
argues for, and second, Paul Tillich's God as the universal ground of human
being also demonstrates how God or the sacred realm deeply and integrally

transform the principalities and powers under the evil scheme and centered at those institutions.[24] Furthermore, King assures us that the universal God has always been on the side of justice and the same God will fight against the forces of evil with us on the battlefield of human history. Surely it is within history that the power of God defeats evil.[25] This is exactly why King preaches:

> Looking back, we see the forces of segregation gradually dying on the seashore. The problem is far from solved and gigantic mountains of opposition lie ahead, but at least we have left Egypt, and with patient yet firm determination we shall reach the promised land. Evil in the form of injustice and exploitation shall not survive forever. A Red Sea passage in history ultimately brings the forces of goodness to victory, and the closing of the same waters mark the doom and the destruction of the forces of evil. All this reminds us that evil carries the seed of its own destruction. In the long run right defeated is stronger than evil triumphant.[26]

King is more than confident that all evil is ultimately doomed by the powerful, inexorable forces of good in the process of human history.[27] Thus, we humans can create a new eschatological community in history under God's goodness. This community will be totally different from the present one, which is polluted with social injustice, racism, sexism, imperial hegemony, unjust wars, political iniquity, etc. King proclaims this new eschatological community "the Beloved Community."[28]

It is well-known that King's eschatology is a social eschatology. His conception of the Kingdom of God is not rooted in the

---

permeates the worldly realm of human existence itself. Further, Boston personalism also helps King advocate the integral worldview as long as personalism argues for the God who personally joins humanity as a loving ally, thus bridging the gap between the spiritual and the secular.

24. Wink, *Engaging the Powers*, 5–10.

25. Erskine, *King among the Theologians*, 145.

26. King, *Strength to Love*, 82–83.

27. King, *Strength to Love*, 78.

28. Broderick and Meier, *Negro Protest Thought*, 272.

image of an otherworldly realm where all children of God share eternal peace, but rather in the image of the *present* world. King describes the zenith of his imagination of this earthly Kingdom as the beloved community, wherein people from all ethnicities share *agape* in eternal peace. This Kingdom of God is possible in this world only because a personal, just, and universal God has already been proclaimed throughout human history, and that same God is helping us to work toward a truly peaceful reality.

Of course, there is no fixed time in human history by which we can be certain this Kingdom of God, or the eschatological hope of a beloved community, will be achieved. Rather, the Kingdom of God is still being established among us through our cooperative proclamation. Indeed, King perceives the Kingdom of God as an ongoing *dream*, which propels us to ceaselessly resist violence and injustice in order to create some version of God's beloved community in this present world. He writes:

> The dream is one of equality of opportunity, of privilege and property widely distributed; a dream of a land where men [sic] will not take necessities from the many to give luxuries to the few; a dream of a land where men do not argue that the color of a man's skin determines the content of his character; a dream of a place where all our gifts and resources are held not for ourselves alone but as instruments of service for the rest of humanity . . . where every man will respect the dignity and worth of all human personality, and men will dare to live together as brothers . . . Whenever it is fulfilled, we will emerge from the bleak and desolate midnight of man's inhumanity to man into the bright and glowing daybreak of freedom and justice for all of God's children.[29]

Once again, this dream is only possible thanks to a God who resists the evil of the present world with our cooperation. Indeed, this resisting God is the theological foundation of the beloved community's creation. King assures us that God's Kingdom is definitely

---

29. King, "The Rising Tide of Racial Consciousness," 4.

coming to overturn the present violent world; in fact, this God has been working *here and now* with us for that purpose.

## The Preacher, Preaching, and the Pulpit Reflected in King

Traditionally, blacks have an image of the black preacher as a prophet. Of course, nowadays there are several other images of the black preacher—such as evangelist, storyteller, proclaimer, herald, social activist, and the like. However, the prophetic image or voice of the black preacher remains dominant in most black churches, whether traditional or contemporary.[30] What then does the prophetic image or prophetic voice refer to in the black church context? In general, the prophetic voice consists of at least three important elements:[31] (a) God's words proclaimed to human decadence such as social injustice and unjust wars; (b) God's or Jesus's irresistible power to overturn those corrupt earthly situations; and (c) the celebration of God's salvation of his people and of the new world (or God's Kingdom) created through that cosmic liberation.

In previous chapters, we have seen that these prophetic elements of preaching are well integrated into King's own preaching. King was very critical in analyzing the socio-political perils that American society was facing and he was faithful in proclaiming God's irresistible power and love to overturn human decadence. Lastly, his preaching celebrated God's victory, God's salvation of people, and the new world (which is the Beloved Community) created by that liberation and salvation. In this respect, we may contend that the image of prophet is most fitting in describing King as a black preacher.

Nonetheless, the prophet image alone is insufficient in depicting King as a preacher when we are reminded of the ultimate goal of King's preaching—that is, the reconciliation of the oppressed and the oppressors. As mentioned earlier, King's eventual goal is

30. Hicks, *The Man Nobody Knows*, 116–18.

31. Mitchell, *Black Preaching*. See chapter 9 "Toward a Theology of Preaching."

not merely the liberation of the oppressed, but ultimate reconciliation between two conflicting parties in the sacrificial love of Christ.[32] This is why King's preaching is not simply the celebration of God's victory over evil, but *the celebration of the universal reconciliation* between God and people *and* between the oppressed and the oppressors. In accordance with this, King preaches:

> The acceptable year of the Lord is that year when men learn to live together as brothers . . . The acceptable year of the Lord is that year when every valley shall be exalted, and every mountain will be made low; the rough places would be made plain, and the crooked places straight; and the glory of the Lord shall be revealed, and all flesh shall see it together . . . Now there is a final reason I think that Jesus says, "Love your enemies." It is this: that love has within it a redemptive power. And there is a power there that eventually transforms individuals. That's why Jesus says, "Love your enemies" . . . So love your enemies.[33]

In the words above we see how King's preaching centers on the matter of reconciliation rooted in love that embraces even our enemies. Here the prophetic image does not serve quite so well.[34] Of course, this does not mean that King cannot be depicted as a prophet at all. Indeed, James Cone already used the prophet image in describing King a couple of decades ago.[35] I only argue here that

32. Erskine, *King among the Theologians*, 127.

33. Erskine, *King among the Theologians*, 112–13, 154.

34. Brueggemann, *The Prophetic Imagination*, 27. Walter Brueggeman states that the common primary "task of prophetic ministry is to nurture, nourish, and evoke a consciousness and perception alternative to the consciousness and perception of the dominant culture around us," but not to pursue the immediate reconciliatory work. Of course, this does not mean that the prophetic task entirely excludes the work of reconciliation. It only means that the reconciliatory task is secondary. In King's case, however, the reconciliatory task would, in fact, seem to be the first priority and governing principle of his social ministry, based on which his prophetic voice of judgment and liberation arises.

35. Garrow, *Martin Luther King, Jr.*, 229. However, in Cone's understanding of King as the prophet, the theme of the prophet as the universal reconciler

describing King only as a prophet does not do him justice. Rather, I propose the image of *prophetic mediator* as the most fitting description for King.

As discussed, King's preaching message centers on the celebration of the universal reconciliation between God and people as well as between the oppressed and the oppressors. As a preaching mediator, King himself stands in between God and the people and between the oppressed and the oppressors.[36] However, his role is not simply to keep standing between two conflicting parties and to wait for them to come together in the middle. Instead, he first listens to God, interprets church tradition (including the Bible), experiences God's transforming and reconciling love himself, and then stands amidst conflicting people to proclaim the reconciliatory message of God. Lastly, he lives the reconciliatory life himself, directly confronting human perils. This is why he can be considered both prophet and mediator. As a prophetic mediator, he is first drawn to God by the reconciliatory message and then, in turn, draws people to the place of universal mediation.

So King, as the mediating preacher, lives in two worlds simultaneously, putting one foot in the realm of God to listen to God's message and the other in the earthly realm to actively engage in it. However, as his eschatology implies, the realm of God, which is the Kingdom of God, is being achieved not in the spiritual world, but here on earth, by transforming the land and creating universal reconciliation between God and people and oppressed and oppressor.

For the prophetic mediator, wherever there is conflict there is also a pulpit. This means that the church is not the only place where the preacher should stand and preach. Rather, the preacher, as a prophetic mediator, is needed everywhere. The pulpit can

---

between God and people and oppressed and oppressors is weak or even absent. Rather, Cone without hesitation interprets King as a prominent demonstrator of the black liberation ideal, even though he still thinks King's reconciliation ideal is by and large mixed up with the white liberal ethos.

36. Of course, in a sense, any prophetic figure would be called a mediator between God and people and between the oppressed and the oppressors, yet again King is different, in placing his active reconciliatory role at the forefront of his public ministry.

be the bus in which Rosa Parks did not yield her seat; it can be Peachtree Rd. in Atlanta where the homeless wander aimlessly; it can be a prison in Birmingham where outcries for justice are heard but ignored; it can be the podium at the Lincoln Memorial where King delivered his "I Have a Dream" speech; or it can be the cheap motel balcony in Tennessee where he was assassinated. Indeed, in a fundamental sense, this kind of pulpit theology makes every place and every moment the place and time for preaching, since all human life is touched by the conflicts between God and humanity and oppressor and oppressed. The racial conflict of King's time is a vivid historical example of that conflict.

Therefore, for King, pulpit ministry—preaching—must go on. There is not, has never been, and will never be a time that we do not sense the two-fold conflicts in our history. Humans, even though they bear the image of God, are sinful in nature, so we always create these conflicts. This sinfulness desperately requires the mediating preacher's reconciliatory message to end the conflict in history and achieve the Kingdom of God, even though evil hinders people from doing the righteous thing.

In King's homiletic theology, the preacher is (and should be) a prophetic mediator who facilitates universal reconciliation not only between God and humanity, but also between the oppressed and the oppressors. People are and always have been in desperate need of this kind of pulpit ministry, because the sinfulness of humanity creates these two-fold conflicts everywhere. King sensed that in the lives of minorities lie vivid instances of that conflict that should be overturned and reconciled in the love of the sacrificed Christ. For this purpose, the preacher's role as a reconciling prophetic mediator will have to continue until the Kingdom of God, the historical counterclaimant to violent reality, is achieved on the earth.

## God Manifested through the Universe as the Counterclaim to a Violent Reality: Violence and Reconciliation

> God has been profoundly real to me in recent years. In the midst of outer dangers I have felt an inner calm. In the midst of lonely days and dreary nights I have heard an inner voice saying, "Lo, I will be with you." When the chains of fear and the manacles of frustration have all but stymied my efforts, I have felt the power of God transforming the fatigue of despair into the buoyancy of hope. I am convinced that the universe is under the control of a loving purpose, and that in the struggle for righteousness man has cosmic companionship. Behind the harsh appearance of the world there is a benign power.[37]

King states that God has always been both an inner force of the oppressed struggling for freedom and justice and an outer transforming power aiming for change in the world. This God is always real to the oppressed and, on their behalf, will fight against violence. As discussed, however, King does not perceive this God as a God of vengeance for the sake of the oppressed. Rather, King knows this God as a God of restoration and reconciliation through the mediation of sacrificial love (*agape*). In particular, this God of reconciliation has been revealed to us personally, biblically, historically, and finally universally.

King had personally experienced this God from the beginning of his public service in Montgomery, Alabama. At the age of twenty-six, King was elected president of the newly formed Montgomery Improvement Association and was chosen to give the black community's response to the arrest of Mrs. Rosa Parks at Holt Church. Almost one-tenth of the black population of Montgomery was there. They listened to the young passionate preacher and did as his speech urged them. To his surprise, as well as many outsiders', his message against the racial and social injustice expressed by Parks's arrest was so powerful, inspiring,

37. King, *Strength to Love*, 153.

and influential, that it felt "as if the twenty six year old had been saying these [powerful] things for many years."[38] That was his first experience of a God who worked *in* and *with* him to fight against injustice and create reconciliation between the oppressed and the oppressors. This God, who cares for the oppressed, would lead and empower King throughout his entire public career. King knew this God to be the counterclaimant to violent reality abiding in him as a source of inner strength. He preaches:

> At that moment I experienced the presence of the Divine as I had never before experienced him. It seems as though I could hear the quiet assurance of an inner voice, saying, "Stand up for righteousness, stand up for truth. God will be at your side forever." Almost at once my fears began to pass from me. My uncertainty disappeared. I was ready to face anything. The outer situation remained the same, but God had given me inner calm.[39]

This passionate and confessional preaching about the personal God seems to be preached to himself. As he mentions repeatedly during his lifetime, he only could persevere in the midst of a variety of cruelty that haunted his life, many times literally, only because this deeply personal God would leave him alone and strengthen him whenever need.

Throughout Scripture King also finds God has been a counterclaimant against violence. The best illustration of this is the Hebrew people's salvation from the Egyptians. King preaches:

> Egypt struggled to maintain her oppressive yoke, and Israel struggled to gain freedom . . . As soon as the Egyptians got into the dried up sea, the parted waters swept back upon them, and the turbulence and momentum of the tidal waves soon drowned all of them . . . Rather, this story symbolizes the death of evil and of inhuman oppression and unjust exploitation.[40]

38. Lischer, *Preacher King*, 85.
39. King, *Strength to Love*, 114.
40. King, *Strength to Love*, 78–79.

For King, the oppressed situation of black people today is very like that of the Israelites in Egypt. Just as God crushed the evil power of Egypt on behalf of the Hebrew people, the current oppression of black people, no doubt, would be shattered by the mighty power of God in the future.

However, King marked one important difference between the liberation of black people and that of the Hebrew people. While there is no active love expressed in Exodus by the Hebrew people toward their enemies, King's comrades are to be commended for their reconciliatory love toward their oppressors. Black Christians are expected to love this way because the crucified Jesus showed that love of one's enemy was the most powerful method of transformation. Besides, King knew that in love there is a redemptive power that eventually transforms sinful individuals.

So, following Jesus, King preaches, "Let us love our enemies."[41] This is the most influential, permanent way we can resist violence. Of course, we ourselves are not the initial subjects of this kind of resistance. God has already initiated this kind of redemptive love and history throughout the Bible. We are the followers of God's way, particularly Jesus's way of transforming the world. Therefore, we cannot be defeated because God, the most Almighty, works in and with us for this resisting, liberating, and transforming work on the streets.

Historically, King finds many cases in which God is shown as the counterclaimant to violent reality by working through God's faithful people. In his sermon, "The Death of Evil upon the Seashore," King narrates how God has worked in U.S. history for black liberation. The first case is that of Thomas Jefferson. By quoting Jefferson's own words, "But the momentous question [slavery], like a fire-bell in the night, awakened and filled me with terror,"[42] King preaches that "numerous abolitionists, like Jefferson, were tortured in their hearts by the question of slavery."[43] The second and most significant case is that of Abraham Lincoln. By drafting

41. King, *Strength to Love*, 49–57.
42. King, *Strength to Love*, 81.
43. King, *Strength to Love*, 81.

the Emancipation Proclamation, which "brought an end to chattel slavery,"[44] Lincoln confirmed and reaffirmed God's work for the oppressed as the unyielding historical counterclaimant to the violent reality of black slavery.

The most recent and dramatic case is that of the Civil Rights Act of 1964, which was a landmark piece of legislation in the United States that outlawed racial segregation in schools, public places, and employment. The fact that all forms of segregation had been declared unconstitutional by the Supreme Court by 1968 was an immeasurable victory for a God working for his oppressed people. Thus, King is bold enough to proclaim and preach that "looking back, we see the forces of segregation gradually dying on the seashore . . . A Red Sea passage in history ultimately brings the forces of goodness to victory, and the closing of the same waters marks the doom and destruction of the forces of evil."[45] Therefore, there is no doubt that King sees God working in history for the liberation of God's people to the very point of evil's ultimate eschatological doom.

Finally, King perceives God's liberating act for God's oppressed people as a universal truth claim against the violent reality of oppression, injustice, and racial segregation. King knows that God's love and justice are the very ground of the universe's existence, although humans have tried to distort or destroy that love and justice through their sinful nature. God is undefeatable and unyielding in planting love and doing justice through faithful people in history. In this respect, the universal character of God's liberating act for God's oppressed people is the first and inclusive aspect of four other characteristics discussed: personal, biblical, christological, and historical.

King, then, realizes that the God revealed through the universe is the Creator and Initiator of the original and true reconciliation between God and people and between oppressed and oppressors. Thus, he preaches, "Above all, we must be reminded anew that God is at work in his universe . . . Here on all the roads

44. King, *Strength to Love*, 81–82.

45. King, *Strength to Love*, 83.

of life, he is striving in our striving. Like an ever-loving Father, he is working through history for the salvation of his children. As we struggle to defeat the forces of evil, the God of the universe struggles with us."[46]

46. King, *Strength to Love*, 84.

# 3

# Invention of *Other*-Typological Illustration: An Analysis of King's Sermon on Exodus 14:30[1]

*Let us remember that as we struggle against Egypt, we must have love . . .*[2]

THIS CHAPTER PROVIDES A close look at one of King's sermons that fully embodies his aforementioned preaching theology of universal reconciliation, specifically an analysis of how he cleverly designs his Exodus sermon in order to maximize his universal reconciliatory message. For this purpose, this chapter explores King's *illustrative* understanding of the Exodus story in his sermon, which demonstrates a stark contrast vis-à-vis the black church's widely accepted *typological* understanding of the same story.[3]

1. The sermon with the title "The Death of Evil upon the Seashore" is found in King, *Papers of Martin Luther King, Jr.*, vol. III, 256–62, as preached at the Cathedral of St. John the Divine on May 17, 1956, New York City. Another published version of the same sermon, revised and expanded, is found in King, *Strength to Love*, 77–86. Between the two there is no major differences found. Yet, I choose to read the first one since it seems to reflect better his theological reconciliatory idea, one of his lifetime sermonic subjects.

2. King, *Papers*, vol. 3, 261.

3. Raboteau, *A Fire in the Bones*. In particular, in chapter 2 Raboteau recognizes that from the early stage of black Christianity the old Israel's Exodus

As we shall see, however, King's illustrative use of the Exodus story is not "pure," but rather takes on a blended form of typology and illustration. King initially embarks on a *different typological* or *other-typological* understanding of the same Exodus story and eventually ends up using that story as a crucial illustration of his sermonic point about universal reconciliation. We will see that all this discussion of typology and illustration is not a simple matter of a different interpretive strategy—which approaches the same story and its same literary-theological meaning merely from a different perspective—but is a significant matter of a different theological understanding of God, humanity, evil, and eschatological ethics, as well as a different literary perception of the Exodus story.

For this investigation, the chapter first provides brief definitions of literary typology and sermon illustration as the critical guide or foundation for the discussion to come. The chapter, with those definitions in hand, then examines how the North American black church, throughout its ecclesial tradition, often has understood the Exodus story in a typological sense for the church's own historical and theological merits.[4] In particular, our focus will go to how black preachers have explicitly demonstrated this typological understanding of the story in their sermons on Exodus, especially for its relevance to black freedom and liberation. For this part of the chapter, I owe a significant investigative debt to Raboteau's historical examination of the typological understanding of the Exodus story in the black church and LaRue's survey of black church sermons in the nineteenth and twentieth centuries.[5]

---

story became a "Black Exodus" story by the "Black Israel" almost in a literal sense; the white America or the new Pharaoh's Egypt was now doomed and would be crushed literally by the mighty God soon. As we will discuss later, however, this literal sense has been weakened since then and indeed replaced rather by a spiritual or metaphoric sense.

4. Black churches are found around the world, including in Latin America, Africa, Europe, etc., with particular historical backgrounds and different theological nuances, and certain commonalities shared. Given the time and space limit, this paper's scope only covers the North American black church context where Dr. King's theology was born and active.

5. Raboteau, *A Fire in the Bones* and LaRue, *The Heart of Black Preaching*.

Then, my writing explores how King demonstrates his unique *other*-typological understanding of the Exodus story away from the traditional one. This critical exploration will in turn lead us to see how King adopts the illustrative use of the story at a certain point of his sermon based on his particular perception of the Exodus narrative.

The last portion of the chapter consists of a close examination of King's illustrative use of the Exodus story in the sermon on Exodus 14:30 anchored in his theological worldview of reconciliation. As we shall see, his particular use of the Exodus story and his theology of reconciliation are symbiotically inseparable. Thanks to the illustrative understanding of the Exodus story, King was able to find a firm theological ground for the God of reconciliation, while the reconciliatory notion of God was exactly his theological hermeneutic that he initially brought to the Exodus text itself.

This chapter dare not state that this narrow investigation on only one of King's sermons will completely explain his sophisticated other-typological or illustrative use of the Exodus story and related complex theological ideas demonstrated in his other sermons and public speeches. Such a task would certainly require volumes of work. Nonetheless, it is my sincere hope that this research on the black church's—and definitely King's—biblical narrative for its faith (i.e., the Exodus), will shed an important interpretative light on King's preaching and his reconciliatory theological worldview, because it is upon this narrative that the black church's theological identity has been built from its inception.[6]

## Definitions: Typology and Illustration

### *Typology*

We need to clarify certain definitions of typology and illustration since they are the key terms hereafter in the chapter, and understanding them correctly—or at least sharing the same definitions—will reduce the risk of misunderstanding the same subjects to come.

6. Mays, *The Negro's God*, 19ff.

*The Cambridge Dictionary of Christianity* defines "typology" as, "a method of interpreting Scripture in which it is assumed that events, institutions, and persons in the OT ('type') foreshadow events, institutions, and persons in the NT, and/or such features of both the OT and the NT foreshadow events, institutions, and persons in the time of the interpreter."[7] What is particularly important for us in the definition is that through the biblical or theological process of typology, people find certain typological counter features of the present (they believe) prefigured in the Old Testament and/or the New Testament. In short, what happened before happens here and now.

Yet, of course, there cannot be any one-to-one correlation of events in a literal sense between what happened before and what is happening now. For instance, when people in the black church tradition interpret the old Exodus story as the anti-type of their modern slavery liberation movement, features of the narrative such as the Red Sea, Pharaoh, the promised land, manna, etc., cannot literally match what the black community has gone through, but they can match *typologically* (e.g., black slaves confronted white masters, but not "modern Pharaoh" in a literal sense).[8]

Furthermore, and more importantly, interpretations of the same typological story can largely vary (or be greatly different from each other), depending on key contemporary typological counterparts that the present reader chooses to bring to the original type features. For instance, as we shall see later in King's case, when King holds up the *universal* American social ills or evils as the typological counterpart of slavery in Egypt—vis-à-vis

---

7. Patte, *Cambridge Dictionary of Christianity*, 946.

8. Binckes, *The Great Trek Uncut*. It should be noted that this sort of typological reading of the Exodus story was not a "new invention" by the North American black church. There were certain precedents in different parts of the world. For instance, Boers (and certainly a good number of blacks in South Africa) held the Exodus narrative as their primary source of inspiration based on which they made their own "Exodus" to eastern and north-eastern areas of South Africa. In the case of Boers, their interpretation and action was closer to literal application, yet still in a typological sense. Binckes, *The Great Trek Uncut*.

the white America that the black tradition has often perceived as the real typological Egyptian enemy—King's eventual interpretive meaning of the same story is thoroughly different from the latter.

## Illustration

According to Thomas G. Long, from approximately the nineteenth century on, there have been two major homiletic streams in understanding illustration, the second stream being more contemporary.[9] The first, somehow pragmatic stream, understands illustrations as "windows on the word" that provide the clarification of logical sermonic concepts. In other words, the sermon will use the illustrations in order to "make the [sermon's] message clear,"[10] "to make the truth concrete,"[11] and eventually "to help the congregation understand"[12] the main ideas of the sermon. Long argues that the use of this utilitarian trend of illustration is widely accepted when and where the sermon is "supposed to develop a 'thesis,' and illustrations [are] seen as devices designed to illuminate and clarify that thesis."[13]

The second stream, which Long strongly advocates for, perceives illustrations as the literary homiletic sinews intrinsically intermingled with the sermon's point. At times, it is so interwoven that, as Fred B. Craddock argues, "[i]n good preaching what is referred to as illustrations are, in fact, stories or anecdotes which do not illustrate the point; rather *they are the point*."[14] Craddock

---

9. Long, *Witness of Preaching*, 200.

10. Sanster, *Craft of the Sermon*, 206. In the black church traditions, the homiletic practice of using illustrations that make "the message clear" is widely known and often utilized. See Mitchell, *Black Preaching*, chap. 4; Cone, *The Spirituals and the Blues*, chap. 3; Proctor, *The Certain Sound of the Trumpet*, chap. 4, and others.

11. Jones, *Principles and Practice*, 137.

12. Sweazey, *Preaching the Good News*, 193.

13. Long, *Witness of Preaching*, 211.

14. Craddock, *Preaching*, 204; italics inserted.

continues, "a story may carry in its bosom the whole message."[15] Long contends that this trend of illustration use has been recently popular with the understanding of the sermon as the "integrated act of communication."[16] In this act, each part of the sermon, including the illustrations, works together in order to achieve one communicational purpose. Illustrations, thus, are not mere "windows" to assist other important parts, but are the important parts themselves.

I purposefully take the first stream of the illustration understanding as the main domain for the rest of the article, not because the former is more appropriate or important in preaching in general, but only because the sermon in focus that we will investigate in following sections operates in that first stream and uses illustrations accordingly.

## Typology: God Only on One Side

From the embryonic stage of black Christianity in America, black Christians have often identified themselves with ancient Israel.[17] That is, just as the Israelites, in the power of YHWH-God, had broken the bondage of Egypt and marched toward the promised land, Christian slaves believed that they too would break the enslaving

15. Craddock, *Preaching*, 204.

16. Long, *Witness of Preaching*, 203.

17. Note that by black Christianity I do not mean one homogenous group of black Christians. Like any other racial-ethnic churches in the U.S. (including Euro-American churches), various denominational branches have existed in the black church from the beginning, which have demonstrated different theological or spiritual themes and emphases even regarding the idea of the "old Israel." See footnote 6 in chapter 1. Also, Lincoln and Mamiya, *The Black Church in the African-American Experience*, esp. chaps 2–4. Lincoln and Mamiya introduce seven historical black denominations, which include the African American Methodist Episcopal Church (A.M.E.), the African Methodist Episcopal Zion church (A.M.E.Z.), the Christian Methodist Episcopal (C.M.E.), the National Baptist Convention, U.S.A., Incorporated (NBC), the National Baptist Convention of America, Unincorporated (NBCA), the Progressive National Baptist Convention (PNBC), and the Church of God in Christ (COGIC).

yoke of the new Egypt and march toward the new promised land.[18] For them, the new Egypt was white America, where their most basic rights were trodden upon by the slave master's brutal iron feet. In that lifeless circumstance, just like the children of Israel, they pursued and proclaimed their freedom and liberation against white America, their evil enemy. A God of power and ultimate good would support and guide this new black Israel's struggle toward the triumphal march into the new Promised America. Definitely, in this new version of the same Exodus story, God is *only on their side* against the evil other.

The black preachers who shared the experience of white American slavery were the *avant-garde* of that new black Israel's struggle against the new American Pharaoh's slave regime. They firmly believed in the typological narrative that God would take their side against the evil counterpart even to the extent that God would help them utterly crush the latter. The same Exodus narrative of the Bible had to be achieved here and now in the new, typological, American history.

Francis J. Grimke (1850–1937), who was regarded as one of the most influential black preachers of his era and helped found the NAACP,[19] is a good example of a person who took this kind of typological understanding of the Exodus story and preached accordingly.[20] In a sermon entitled, "A Resemblance and a Contrast between the American Negro and the Children of Israel, in Egypt, or the Duty of the Negro to Contend Earnestly for his Rights

18. Raboteau, *Fire in the Bones*, 28. Of course, as Raboteau recognizes throughout the book, today's black Christianity, approximately after the sixties civil rights movements, identifies itself less with the old Israel than the eighteenth or nineteenth century's counterpart did, since black Christians no longer live in the old slave market era. Yet, the same "Black Exodus" motif still remains in the black church's "bones" and often becomes the key subject of black preaching today because the ongoing racial discrimination, implicit or explicit, is considered the extension of the old black slavery era.

19. NAACP stands for the National Association for the Advancement of Colored People, the non-profit organization whose Atlanta branch King's father headed and which King joined in the late fifties and with which he once had an influential role.

20. LaRue, *The Heart of Black Preaching*, 46.

Guaranteed under the Constitution," Grimke preaches on Exodus
1:9–10:

> When the children of Israel first went down into Egypt
> it was with no intention of remaining there permanently
> . . . Nor was it in accordance with the divine plan that
> they should remain permanently, as is evident from the
> record, in forty-six of Genesis. "And God spake into Is-
> rael in the vision of the night, and said, Jacob, Jacob . . .
> fear not to go down into Egypt, for I will there make of
> thee a great nation: I will go down with thee into Egypt,
> and I will surely bring thee up again." God is not dead—
> nor is He an indifferent onlooker at what is going on in
> this world . . . If some Moses should rise up today, as
> of old, and say to this nation, as was said to Pharaoh,
> "Let my people go" . . . I believe from every part of the
> land—North, South, East, and West, there would be but
> one voice, and that would be, Let them go . . . One day He
> will make requisition for blood; He will call the oppres-
> sors to account . . . If we are true to ourselves and to God
> the victory will be ours.[21]

As explicated above, the preacher demonstrates several typological understandings of both the Exodus story and black Christians.
First, black Christians are chosen people just as the people of Jacob
were chosen by the sovereign God. Second, God is mighty enough
to deliver them from the current bondage of slavery just as the
God of Exodus did for the Israelites. Third, black people, just as the
Israelites, will be the ultimate victors of this struggle against the
ruthless oppressors of slavery. Finally, God's judgment is coming
just as it did for ancient Israel. In short, the old familiar Exodus
story *becomes* black people's story. That is, Israel's Exodus story has
become the *black Exodus* story.

This typological understanding eventually leads black
Christianity to the celebration of liberation, along with a story in
which God is on their side. Of course, since God is the God of
all creation, the evil oppressors also exist within God's sovereign
reign and have a chance to be included into the liberation of the

---

21. Woodson, *Works of Francis J. Grimke*, vol. 1, 348–56.

oppressed. Yet, as long as their evil conduct goes on, and they do not repent, they have no chance to be included in God's new promised land, but are doomed to die on the seashore. Nor are liberated black people supposed to have compassion and love for their resisting, stiff-necked enemies just doomed to death. As a black slave woman from late nineteenth-century America prays out loud for a divine retaliation:

> Thar's day a comin'! Thar's a comin . . . I hear de rumblin' ob de chariots! I see de flashin' ob de guns! White folks' blood is a runnin' on de ground like a riber, an' de dead's heaped up dat high! . . . Oh, Lor'! hasten de day when de blows, an' de bruises, an' de aches, an' de pains, shall come to de white folks, an' de buzzards shall eat 'em as dey's dead in de streets. Oh, Lor'! roll on de chariots, an' gib de Black people rest an' peace.[22]

As the prayer goes, the ultimate celebration only belongs to one final victorious side of the black people, while the counter "white folks" are utterly doomed. Yet again, as indicated above, there is still a chance for oppressors to repent, return, and enjoy God's salvation alongside the currently oppressed blacks; however, the "chance" will not last forever. Repentance is an urgent matter.[23]

In sum, the traditional,[24] typological understanding of the Exodus story explicitly delineastes two sides between the good-oppressed and evil-oppressor, and God solely as a God of the oppressed.[25] Obviously, this God of the oppressed is a God of

22. Livermore, *My Story of the War*, 260–61.

23. As we will see later, however, the matter of repentance as the primary task gives way to the more foundational matter of evil exorcism in King's theology.

24. From this point on, when my article uses the phrase "traditional understanding" or "typical understanding" of the Exodus story, I will only mean that this typological understanding has been widely accepted in the black church from the church's very inception in America, as Mays finds out in his *The Negro's God*. As Mays also finds out, and as will be discussed below again, however, this will not mean that not all black Christians have shared this traditional or typical understanding.

25. Cilliers, *God for Us*, 1–5. In an intercultural comparison sense, it is interesting to know that during apartheid in South Africa, white Afrikaners

retributive justice who is willing to defeat and even crush the enemies "at the seashore." The eventual freedom and liberation belong to enslaved black people only. Therefore, in the conventional black Exodus narrative, there is no grand anticipation of potential reconciliation between the two opposing sides, *unless there is repentance first on the side of the oppressors.*[26]

## Other-Typology: God on Both Sides

It is very likely that King fully recognized this traditional typological understanding of the Exodus story. For he grew up in the typical black Baptist church where the dramatic story of the prophet-liberator Moses was told as one of the central prophetic identities of the black preacher.[27] King himself kept this prophet-

---

believed and even preached the theological idea of "God is for us." According to Johan Cilliers, they identified themselves as ancient Israel in a typological sense. As God defended and fought against all other nations who attacked old Israel, white Afrikaner preachers preached that God would defend them and fight against rebellious blacks. In this instance, God "belongs to" only one (white) side.

26. Baer and Singer, *African American Religion*, chaps. 1 and 2. As mentioned in passing above, not all black Christians have shared the typological story of Exodus and thus the typological narrative identity in faith, namely "God-with-only-us" faith. Indeed, throughout black church history, there have been a considerable number of black churches that did not express this dichotomous understanding of God and the world, and rather took an accommodationist position either voluntarily or by slavery brainwashing, in which they would accept the faith type of "God-with-them-as well." Baer and Singer, even though their focus is not on the typological narrative understanding of the black church itself, indicate this point well. According to them, this somehow compromised, but not necessarily reconciliatory, socio-theological position of the black church already appeared early in the black church's inception, though weak at that time. Eventually, this second position grew stronger, even though still remaining a minority group in the black church, influenced in particular by advanced industrial capitalism in and from the late nineteenth century. Thus, at this point it would suffice to remember that not all black church branches have kept the typological narrative identity with the "God-with-only-us" faith based on the Exodus story.

27. Lischer, *Preacher King*, 173. During ane interview with Lischer, a retired beautician and member of Ebenezer still refers to King as "a Moses to the Black race."

Moses image as one of his prominent personas, utilized effectively for his public ministry.[28]

Thus, it is no wonder that in his sermon on Exodus 14:30, King seems at first to follow the typological narrative ethos and pathos of the Exodus story. He tells us from the middle of the sermon that the evils of segregation, oppression, and colonialism that black people are now facing are the same evils that Egypt and its Pharaoh symbolized and imposed on the Hebraic people. And just as the evil of the slavery-obsessed Pharaoh died at the seashore, we are now also gradually seeing the death of segregation and oppression in the sheer dawn of freedom and justice. At this point, therefore, it seems that King well pictures the current social situation of black people in a typological sense; that is, black people's liberation story is equivalent to the Exodus liberation story.

Yet, we notice that King's typological interpretation of the Exodus story above already subtly breaks away from the black church's common typological understanding of the same story— even though his sermon goes on in similar typological narrative form and tone. King, unlike the traditional typological perception, does not equate the evils of Egypt or Pharaoh with white America itself. Rather, he uses those anti-types of evil in order to designate bigger or universal American social problems that black people are now confronting: segregation, oppression, colonialism, etc. Changing the "face of the enemy" from white America to American social ills (or evils), even though it seems to be a little thing, makes a huge difference in the typological understanding of the Exodus narrative. In this new typological understanding, white America would no longer be the very enemy to be crushed; rather, as his sermon later insists, they can be reconciled and included in God's universal favor. At this point we see a new, different typological understanding of the Exodus story start to emerge in King's sermon.

At the end of the sermon, again King suddenly and explicitly breaks out of the traditional, typological understanding of the black Exodus story of liberation by saying, "Let us remember

---

28. Lischer, *Preacher King*, 174–75; 225.

that as we struggle against Egypt, we must have love, compassion, and understanding goodwill for those against whom we struggle, helping them to realize that as we seek to defeat the evils of Egypt we are not seeking to defeat them but to help them, as well as ourselves."[29] Now King is saying that his listeners should not want to defeat their evil enemies but instead to "help them." More than that, his listeners should have "love, compassion, and understanding goodwill" for those who have oppressed them.

This is obviously not the expected end of the common typological understanding of the black Exodus. Even the evil enemies now seem to be able to be fully included on God's side, which certainly makes the traditional typological understanding of the Exodus story pretty unreliable; for the latter understanding sees evildoers' ultimate doom at the seashore (again, unless there is repentance from the latter). Yet, as said before, it is not that King's argument operates totally outside of the typological frame of the Exodus story. He still maintains a similar form and tone to the typological narrative of the black church, but at the same time subverts the fundamental ethos and pathos—thus generating an *other*-typological interpretation.

For King, this sudden and explicit breakout from the traditional typological story line is inevitable for one fundamental theological reason. King, as we shall discuss later more in detail, recognizes reconciliation between the two opposing sides as the ultimate socio-theological end of the black struggle against all kinds of social evil. He says in his own words, "God has a great plan for this world. His purpose is to achieve a world where all men will live together as brothers, and where every man recognizes the dignity and worth of all human personality."[30] The common typological understanding of the Exodus story cannot convey this message as King intends because it primarily seeks black liberation, but not necessarily communal reconciliation, which King firmly believes is a higher goal to be achieved. For King, this ultimate reconciliation is possible, and indeed desired, because

29. King, *Papers*, vol. 3, 261.
30. King, *Papers*, vol. 3, 262.

of his particular theological understanding of humanity, or more specifically evildoers; that is, his theological anthropology that is very different from the counterpart found in the traditional typological narrative of the Exodus story.

In the latter, black Exodus narrative, the evil of the universe very much equals the evildoers of slavery. There is no separation between the two. So, as the universal evil must be defeated, the evildoers must be utterly crushed because both are the same. Contrariwise, in King's theological anthropology as demonstrated in his sermon, evildoers are not perceived as evil itself; rather they are *ignorant victims or unfortunate counter-slaves* captured in the universal evil scheme. Thus, while universal evil must be defeated, the unfortunate, white, evil-performers must be freed and liberated as well. In short, the evil-performers themselves are not evil objects doomed to destruction. Furthermore, the prerequisite for reconciliation is not repentance of ignorant victims (which will follow later), but "exorcism" of the cosmic evil that has polluted their hearts and minds.

In sum, as a good student of the typological Exodus understanding, King initially absorbs the black tradition's typological ethos and pathos in its full sense; the evil against the black liberation must be defeated. Changing the very face of the evil itself, however, King generates a new, different typological perception of the same story that I would like to call *other*-typology. Yes, the evil of the contemporary Egypt and Pharaoh must be defeated, but the evil is not white America itself (or white people); rather the evil's identity is the universal social illness permeating American soil. King believes that when this social evil is defeated, there must be grand reconciliation between the oppressed (black people) and the oppressors (white people).

## Toward the Exodus Illustration, Theological-Rhetorical

In this section, we discuss how King, in light of his understanding of the Exodus typology, uses the story as the best available illustration to support the reconciliatory point of his sermon message. In other words, we will see that King is utilizing the Exodus story as the best case for presenting the key sermon point more clearly and persuasively; certainly, then, the old familiar Exodus story ceases to be the traditional typological story of black life now and then. As we will see, however, this illustrative use of Exodus is only possible because King invents the other-typological understanding of the story first.

In order to examine how King utilizes the Exodus story as a good illustration of the sermon point, we need to see the whole picture of the sermon and outline the flow of it, since the story appears as a critical illustrative part of the sermon.[31] Here is the basic literary scheme of the sermon:

1. Evil is present in the universe.

2. The Bible affirms the reality of evil.

3. Our everyday life also confirms the reality of evil.

4. In a sense, the whole history of life is the history of a struggle between good and evil.

5. But, the Hebraic Christian tradition affirms the ultimate doom of evil (for example, Christ's resurrection).

6. The Exodus story is also a graphic example of the final triumph of good over evil, Egypt being the symbol of doomed evil and Israel one of victorious goodness.

7. Contemporary examples like the civil rights movement also reveal the ultimate victory of good.

31. My method of sermon analysis partly resonates with the Heidelberg method of sermon analysis, which Cilliers adopts in his analysis of sermons produced during the apartheid period in South Africa (Cilliers, *God for Us*, 11–13). Great merits of this method are that 1) it analyzes the sermon both as a whole and according to meaning blocks; 2) it attempts to see explicit and implicit signs of languages in the sermon; 3) it explores what particular characteristics of God are revealed in the sermon; and 4) it interrogates how the biblical text is used in the making of a situational analogy between the present and the biblical time. I utilize these four (and more) merits in my analysis of King's sermon.

8. This cosmic spiritual reality of ultimate good will eventually transform all corrupt people's minds captured in evil's universal scheme.

9. There is God's great plan for a world where all men will live together as brothers, namely the Kingdom of Christ.

As explicit in the outline, the sermon starts with a general statement of cosmic evil's presence in the universe and then enumerates two areas (or examples) in which that statement is affirmed. What follows next is the second message point that the Christian tradition demonstrates the ultimate doom of evil and victory of universal good, undergirded by three illustrations: Christ's resurrection, the Exodus story, and the contemporary black struggle. Finally, the sermon ends by stating that God has a plan for a reconciled world following the utter destruction of evil, where all people, including former oppressors, will join one another as a divine family. Here, King is clear that this third message point of the sermon is his ultimate vision of the world that he wants others to share as their own new Christian vision, story, and future faith identity for the production of the reconciled reality of the world.

The Exodus story, to which our research focus goes, appears in the sermon as the second illustration of the second message point—the cosmic struggle between good and evil, and the final doom of the latter and the victory of the former. As said above, this second sermon point is not the ultimate message nor can the Exodus story itself convey what King ultimately wants to proclaim. Simply put, the victory of one side and the doom of the other is not what King eventually seeks; he wants more than that. King pictures the second sermon point along with its illustrations as a penultimate or prerequisite stage toward the final, more glorious stage of the reconciled world of which he dreams. Going back to the question of the Exodus story itself, it is obvious that at its best, the story remains an important illustration of the second sermon point, but not a traditional typological narrative on which the whole sermonic story line would be based. King himself affirms this in his own words:

> A graphic example of this truth is found in an incident in the early history of the Hebrew people . . . Egypt was the symbol of evil in the form of humiliating oppression, ungodly exploitation and crushing domination . . . This story symbolizes something basic about the universe. It symbolizes something much deeper than the drowning of a few men, for no one can rejoice at the death or the defeat of a human person. This story, at bottom, symbolizes the death of evil. It was the death of inhuman oppression and ungodly exploitation.[32]

King realizes that the Exodus story itself symbolizes or exemplifies a deeper truth that is bigger than what the story itself tells us in a literal or (traditional) typological sense. In other words, at this point, the Exodus story functions as a critical illustration that points to what the sermon ultimately argues for as "something [truthful] in the very nature of the universe."[33] In short, King uses the Exodus story, alongside other illustrations, to provide a foundational sermonic-literary ground for the bigger vision of the defeat of the evil itself and a reconciled world, beyond any simple theme of Exodus-liberation from slavery or socio-political bondage.

Nonetheless, a reasonable question still lingers unresolved around at this point: Why do the readers of King, such as Lischer, still mistakenly think that King was utilizing the Exodus story in a traditional typological sense, even though he was *not*?[34] A probable answer has been given in the previous section, namely, that King invents a new, different *typology*; people tend to take this different typology as the same as the traditional one. Yet, a couple of certain literary—or theological—rhetorical techniques demonstrated in the sermon provide other good, probable reasons to respond to this question as well.

---

32. King, *Papers*, vol. 3, 259–60.

33. King, *Papers*, vol. 3, 260.

34. Lischer, *Preacher King*, 202–12.

First, it is because the Exodus story—even though it does not function at all in the sermon as a traditional typological narrative—still supplies significant symbolic or metaphoric language in which the final sermon point is made. This is very true as the sermon approaches its end, when King preaches, "[God] is seeking at every moment of His existence to lift men from the bondage of some evil Egypt, carrying them through the wilderness of discipline, and finally to the promised land of personal and social integration."[35] In this short statement, there are three important symbols or metaphors working effectively and persuasively: Egypt, the wilderness, and the promised land. Once again, it should be clear that this statement does not, though it seems to, follow the common typological understanding of the Exodus story. Rather, the ultimate vision of the reconciled world in the statement comes from King's *other*-typological reconstruction of the story. That being confirmed, it can be said that, just as King recognizes in the sermon, Egypt symbolizes evil of the universe while the wilderness and the promised land metaphorize the ongoing good-evil struggle and the reconciled world, respectively.[36]

35. King, *Papers*, vol. 3, 260.

36. It is not easy to differentiate symbols from metaphors in any literature as well as in King's sermon because in a linguistic or semiotic sense meanings or literary functions generated by those two literary tropes often overlap even in one literary work. Yet, to speak very briefly in terms of their differences, symbols always have distinctly relatable objects that are symbolized (e.g., The Stars and Stripes is a symbol of nothing but the U.S. nation), while metaphors produce various meanings of objects that are metaphorized depending on the literary situation (e.g., when we say "Time is Money" or "Time is Revelation," these two time metaphors create different literary meanings). In King's sermon in focus, Egypt is symbolized as evil (one-to-one match) and the reconciled world is delineated by several metaphors like the promised land and the Kingdom of the Lord (yet, the promised land itself is not a distinctly relatable symbol of the reconciled community). Nonetheless, as said, just like in many other sermons of King's, sermonic symbols and metaphors in the sermon in focus are often interchanged; that is, at times certain symbols become metaphors and vice versa (e.g., When King says, "Many years ago, the Negro was thrown into the Egypt of segregation. . . ," here the term "Egypt" is used as metaphor rather than as symbol.). For the detailed definition and discussion on symbol and metaphor, see Chandler, *Semiotics: The Basics*, 38–39 and Lakoff and Johnson, *Metaphors We Live By*, 3–6.

Throughout the sermon, especially in the second sermon point of black liberation through Exodus, this symbolic language and similar metaphoric expressions are strong enough to generate the reasonable impression of King's traditional typological understanding of the Exodus narrative. It is as if King were exclaiming, "This story is just like our story!" Yet, as we know now, that Exodus story is not what King depicts as his ideal or his own faith story. The ideal is something else.

Thus, King is not prone to accept the Exodus story itself as his own faith identity. However, at least for King, the Exodus symbolism and related metaphoric expressions are the most, if not best, effective and persuasive literary tools in coining his novel theological ideas that are acceptable to his people who have been traditionally and easily identified with the typological Exodus narrative itself. Indeed, that is how good symbols and metaphors generally work in literature: the generation of the new reality or novel concept of the world with the familiar linguistic or narrative concepts.[37]

Second, King's illustrative interpretation of the Exodus story sounds highly traditional-typological, though it is not, because King first approaches the Exodus story from a cosmic perspective and then applies ethical dimensions of the story to the contemporary world and beyond. On the surface, it seems that King is identifying the black church's contemporary earthly struggle with that of ancient Israelites in Exodus. But, again, this typological understanding of King's use of the Exodus story cannot do full justice to King himself. King, with a different typological and theological ideal that cannot originate from the traditional interpretation of the same story, overcomes the theological limit of the story's ethical lesson. For King, the black church's struggle or its ultimate purpose should be something far beyond the "earthly" resolution between the oppressed and the oppressing reality.

---

37. Lakoff and Johnson, *Metaphors We Live By*, 3–6.

## Conclusion

King's invention of the *different-typological* or *other-typological* understanding of the Exodus story leads to the illustrative use of the same story at a certain point of the sermon. Or the inverse may be true. Because King wants to use the Exodus story as an excellent illustration only for the smaller or preparatory point of the sermon (King has another ultimate point of the sermon), the new typological understanding of the same story was inevitable for the continuing symbolic or metaphoric use up until the end of the sermon. This different typology of the Exodus story and its illustrative use by King rise from his own theological ideal and worldview that the original typological interpretation of the story cannot provide—namely, the victory of universal good over cosmic evil and the resulting reconciliation of all humanity in the presence of one true universal and personal God, who is nothing but the Eternal Beloved.

# 4

## Application of King's Homiletic Theology to the Present World

### Violent Reality, Then and Now

IN HIS 1992 WORK, *Engaging the Powers*, Walter Wink states, "Violence is the ethos of our times. It is the spirituality of the modern world."[1] Nowadays, we experience violence everywhere, even though not every violent case is visible or directly experienced. In his statement, Wink was referring specifically to two aspects of violence that make us particularly uncomfortable or desperate living in a twenty-first-century North American context: the unceasing presence of violence and its spiritual power.

Wink's statement was made twenty-four years after Martin Luther King was assassinated. A great deal had changed over those two decades, yet violence itself had not changed much at all! Violence was still violence. Though when Wink discusses the violent ethos of the modern world, he does not have the civil rights movement at the forefront of his mind (still, he mentions King several times in his writing); his critical observation that our time and place is more permeated with violence is valid and helpful. Wink

---

1. Wink, *Engaging the Powers*, 13.

also observes that human violence has become an acceptable *spirituality* of the modern world. That is, violence has become a *real* part of our souls and lives so that now we not only accept violence as a *natural* part of our life, but also in many cases *approve* of the use of violence.

Of course in the twentieth century, including King's era, violence in various forms was sanctioned in many ways, but now, sadly, we see this tendency elevated even more in everyday life. Indeed, the most dreadful thing about violence is that once we start accepting and approving of it as a natural or inevitable part of our lives, there is no remedy except more violence. Given the circumstance, we (must) ask: In a culture with such a violence-saturated ethos, where do we find hope and what message should be proclaimed? Specifically, what hope or message do we preachers have to proclaim? When these urgent questions visit our troubled hearts, gratefully we may find King's homiletic practice or his pastoral and prophetic message still applicable today for many a great benefit. I see at least three benefits or lessons from King that we can adopt in formulating the message of hope, justice, and reconciliation for our context.

## A Three-Fold Theological and Homiletic Lesson from King

Before delving into a detailed discussion of King's homiletic practice on violence, we need to realize that King was fiercely fighting against the violent culture of his own era. He was not only struggling with the racial issue, which was immediately related to black people's lives; he was also trying to deconstruct all kinds of violence in the modern world—such as economic injustice, socio-political inequity, and immigrants' perils caused by oppressive social and political powers. For instance, one of his biggest concerns regarding the violence of his era was the Vietnam War, in which the U.S. was taking a significant part. He furiously and publicly opposed the Vietnam War because of its unjust causes and the misjudgment of the U.S. about that war. Many citizens were excited about and supported the war, which made King both severely depressed and irritated. He could not accept U.S. citizens' unjust minds and violent actions in the Vietnam War. King preached:

> I am convinced that it is one of the most unjust wars that has ever been fought in the history of world. Our involvement in the war in Vietnam has torn up the Geneva Accord. It has strengthened the military industrial complex; it has strengthened the forces of reaction in our nation. It has put us against the self-determination of a vast majority of the Vietnamese people, and put us in the position of protecting a corrupt regime that is stacked against the poor.[2]

King was troubled by the internal corruption of the U.S. that was exposed outwardly through the Vietnam War, and in turn worsened the internal problem exponentially. The War *had to* be stopped immediately.

Sadly, unjust social matters, political inequity, and other types of violence from King's era continue to exist in ours. In everyday life, we often witness the economic injustice between Hispanic immigrants and their employers; we hear of plans to destroy black churches; we watch cruel killings and other violence on reality T.V. shows and dramas; we witness how unjustly children and women are treated in our society; we read in the morning newspapers about the increasing death toll of and by U.S. soldiers dispatched to other countries; and we hear the news of violent rapes and murders happening every hour in Darfur, Sudan, and around the globe. De facto, we continue to live in the era of violence in which King once lived, which eventually led to his assassination. Therefore, in terms of the cruelty and pervasiveness of violence, there is no cultural difference between his time and ours.

This is why I invite us to revisit preacher King's reconciliatory theology and his preaching messages. His theology and messages still have much to teach us in the twenty-first century. In at least three ways his preaching theology and messages can help us to cope with our own issues of violence.

2. Carson and Holloran, *A Knock*, 219.

## Unveil and Deny the Cultural Ethos of Violence

King guides us to unveil the current cultural ethos of violence and its denial. Just as many did in King's time, so too nowadays we tend to accept and, even worse, approve of the violent cultural ethos of our society, which in turn engenders a great deal of injustice. In other words, we accept and approve of violence without reflecting on it critically. How sad is that! We tend to think that violence is a natural and inescapable thing. We believe it is the way in which humans and society are created to live. "The survival of the fittest," has become a daily mantra. Hence, for instance, we tend to accept as natural that very few people have abundance while most people struggle to get by, or that nations must invade other nations to get more land, resources, and power. By our action or our inaction, we ultimately approve of people with economic and socio-political privileges that monopolize their power.

We have come to believe that this is the natural way to live. Rather than contest the inequality, we accept it, or worse, we actually endorse it. Yet that very kind of thinking regarding social, economic, and political violence King opposed. For him, there is nothing natural about humans being violent toward each other. Indeed, it is a corruption of original human nature created in *imago Dei* (the image of God). According to the Holy Scriptures, specifically the book of Genesis, humans were never created to live in violence. Rather, we were created to live in harmony and peace with each other as well as with God. On that basis, God created the whole universe. The God of universal love and justice created the world for humanity to live in peace, love, and justice with all others, King believed. It is no secret that we are far from living in the way God intended. We fallen humans have corrupted the original Garden of peace and love, instead generating an unnatural violence. To have any chance at recapturing the original nature of this world and our society, thought King, we first have to condemn and deny that corruption and violence.

## Participate in Historical God's Transforming Work

Second, whether Christian or not, King thought we are all invited to participate in God's transforming work in history through everyday life situations. Such partnership and collaboration is crucial. For God does not exist "over there," beyond the mess of the human world, nor is God an abstract projection of humanity's spiritual ideal. Rather, God is *here and now*, working with the oppressed and afflicted for the historical transformation of the unjust human world.

Indeed, this is both (1) a strong counter-cultural statement against the broad societal ethos of atheism today—which tends to make us regard the God of real historical liberation and reconciliation as a God of creative human invention for an imaginary mythic world—and (2) an adamant denial of the current church's supernatural eschatology or so-called "after-death eschatology." Already, capitalist society has lost any notion of divine judgment upon the historical world. In regard to justice, capitalist society knows only its own laws, customs, and regulations. So, when its laws, customs, and regulations justify its ideals of life and social actions, there can be no higher judgment upon it, even though its ideals and actions may be unjust in the light of basic human nature or from any fine religious perspective. In such a society, there is no such thing as the God who acts against its unjust causes.

Unfortunately, nowadays many Christian churches have also abandoned the notion of divine judgment upon human history. The churches seem to be satisfied with after-death eschatology (or Last Day eschatology), as Jürgen Moltmann lamented decades ago.[3] With this type of eschatology, the churches are unable to think about and act for God's historical transformation of oppressive life circumstances. Many churches no longer talk about justice and transformation on the earth in the here and now, but project it to some far off date or far off heavenly place. In so doing, churches do not recognize their own redemptive and transformative capacity, a capacity planted in them long ago and demonstrated in Christ's life, death, and resurrection.

3. Moltmann, *Theology of Hope*, 15–16.

Facing these two misguided social and ecclesial notions on the divine judgment and transformation, King cannot be more unyielding in asserting God's historical judgment upon the violent reality (or the oppressors) and God's historical restoration of the afflicted. Judgment is not the final phase, however. *Ultimately, God works toward reconciliation first between God and people and second between the afflicted and the violent oppressors or systems.* So King reiterates over and over again that God is present now, for and with God's people. King realized that in history there had been a number of vivid examples of God at work in such people and events as Thomas Jefferson, Abraham Lincoln, Sojourner Truth, the Emancipation Proclamation, and the Civil Rights Act of 1964. To his mind, such instances of God's redemptive, transformative, and reconciling work in people's everyday lives is the best example churches today can give of God's participation in the lives of the afflicted, the poor, and the abandoned.

### The Preacher's Pastoral and Prophetic Message

Lastly, King realized that when the church awakens to the violent causes of society, preachers can play a significant role in that transforming and liberating work by preaching pastoral and prophetic messages on the Word of Christ. Indeed, King came to acknowledge this reality by his own experiences in Montgomery. When one third of the city's black population gathered to listen to Reverend King—and when he experienced that his voice was the most powerful cause for the black people's nonviolent liberation movement—King instantly knew that the preacher could play a key role in the liberation of the afflicted blacks. As his life shows, King himself played that key role as a prophetic mediator for reconciliation between God and humans and between afflicted persons and oppressive systems. By being a prophetic mediator for transformation and reconciliation, King created his own pastoral and prophetic message for Christians and all of society. Doubtless, his message was both pastoral and prophetic. Pastorally, he pursued peace, love, and reconciliation of all people; prophetically, he actively invested himself in social transformation.

This is a huge challenge to preachers today. Confronting social injustice and all kinds of violence, we preachers are encouraged and challenged to preach pastorally and prophetically for all people's reconciliation and social transformation. Of course, we preachers are not expected to deliver a pastoral *and* prophetic message all the time. At times, genuine pastoral preaching is required—as in the case of a beloved elder's peaceful funeral service—while for other occasions justice-seeking prophetic preaching is mandatory—as in the case of a Women's Rights March. Yet, in the final analysis, King himself shows that combining the Christian message of agape-oriented human care with adamant social prophecy is the best mode of any preaching for the sake of the suffering violent world.

## Summary

Thankfully, preacher King is still among us. We can refer to him, as well as his many sermons and speeches, as we shape our own pastoral and prophetic messages for transformation and reconciliation in the present violent world. Thus, we are called *here and now*, just as King was, to work for transformation of social violence, for peace and love between conflicting parties, for healing and restoration of the afflicted, and for harmonious life among all nations. To this transformational yearning and continuing pursuit of reconciliation, King seems to have his own theological and homiletic answer to violence that he shares with us: that we should trust, preach, and act in light of the same compassionate God who works for and within us for liberation, peace, justice, and reconciliation of the afflicted in our particular historical contexts today.

# Conclusion

In January 2009, Bishop Woodie W. White, the Bishop in Residence at Candler School of Theology in Emory University then, wrote his 33rd annual letter to King as follows:

> Those days of marches and protests were aimed at simple but important goals: to eat at a lunch counter, to try on a garment before you purchased it, to attend a school in the neighborhood where you lived, to be hired for a job for which you were qualified, and yes, to exercise the most fundamental right of citizenship, to vote . . . We sought to be accepted, and to be treated as a person and a full citizen in our own nation . . . That said, it would be naïve to conclude that racism and bigotry in America are dead. *They are very much alive. Racism dies hard.* But its grip in the minds and hearts of Americans, Martin, is not as deep or as broad as you experienced. . . We need to still challenge every expression of injustice, bigotry and racism in individuals and institutions. Mr. Obama's election should encourage us to continue rather than end these efforts! . . . In so many ways, Martin, we are a better nation, a better people than you left. Not perfect, but better. And in some ways, the nation is moving beyond The Dream! Thank you and happy birthday, Martin. We are overcoming![1] (emphasis inserted)

What Bishop White is telling us through his letter to King is straightforward: King's legacy of the pastoral and prophetic message has continued ever since he left America by his tragic assassination.

1. White, "A Letter to Martin Luther King, Jr."

We are the inheritors and practitioners of King's legacy, challenged to continue King's work and King's dream. In fact, this is what would best serve as the conclusion to my essay. Vis-à-vis the ever-daunting violent reality, King looked to God, who has been proclaimed throughout the universe and has also participated in human history to turn the perils of the afflicted into a Beloved Community of peace, justice, and harmony. King especially found and experienced that God in many historical instances and preached that God in his own present—physical and historical—moment. He was a preacher who *re-represented* that God of peace, care, and justice through his own words.

It was one of King's dreams that every person who experienced the same God that King preached would be able to come together to make the world more peaceful, just, and harmonious. For then, "every valley shall be exalted, and every mountain will be made low; the rough places would be made plain, and the crooked places straight; and the glory of the Lord shall be revealed, and all flesh shall see it together."[2]

In Bishop White's letter to King, we find that King's ambitious dream is being achieved through the people who listened to his words and adopted his dream as their own. Among the many reasons why this has been possible is this: the God that King found is a real participant in human history. This God is a loving Friend of the afflicted and an all-embracing Reconciler between the oppressed and the oppressors. King knew that this God would be a sincere Companion of the oppressed, the poor, and the abandoned until the day when the Beloved Community is achieved in human history. Until then, people's struggle for the salvation of humanity and liberation of the afflicted from violence will continue. Also, until then, the preacher's pastoral and prophetic message will not cease. Preachers will preach the message of reconciliation and justice until God's universal love fills the whole human land, until God's justice rolls down like waters on the earth, and until righteousness like an ever-flowing stream courses through all humans' hearts. King's homiletic dream still breathes among us.

2. Carson and Holloran, *A Knock,* 112–13.

# Appendix

## *A Sermon: "Armageddon Turned Paradise"*

> He shall judge between the nations, and shall arbitrate
> for many peoples; they shall beat their swords into plow-
> shares, and their spears into pruning hooks; nation shall
> not lift up sword against nation, neither shall they learn
> war any more. (Isaiah 2:4)

> The wolf shall live with the lamb, the leopard shall lie
> down with the kid, the calf and the lion and the fatling
> together, and a little child shall lead them. The cow and
> the bear shall graze, their young shall lie down together;
> and the lion shall eat straw like the ox. The nursing child
> shall play over the hole of the asp, and the weaned child
> shall put its hand on the adder's den. They will not hurt
> or destroy on all my holy mountain; for the earth will be
> full of the knowledge of the LORD as the waters cover
> the sea. On that day the root of Jesse shall stand as a sig-
> nal to the peoples; the nations shall inquire of him, and
> his dwelling shall be glorious. (Isaiah 11:6–10)

It was a beautiful, sunny Saturday morning some weeks ago. When
I woke up and pulled up the curtain, I felt strongly that I needed
to go jogging to refresh myself, at least for the sake of the beautiful
weather itself.

From my yet short life experience, I knew that a feeling of that kind was unusual for me since I don't work out as much as I should. I thought there must be some good reason for that good strong compulsion for jogging, so I put on some sport clothes and started running toward a nearby state park.

It was such a beautiful day, as I said, so, when I arrived at the park, breathing heavily, I saw a dozen people already enjoying the shining sky and warm environment of the park. I stopped at the edge of a field, sipped some water from the bottle I carried, and started seeing, feeling, and enjoying the gentle warmth of the day myself. In that peaceful park, I saw two children throwing balls, a mom and dad watching them playing, a dog sniffing around the corner, a fountain springing up in waterfall-like streams, an artist drawing some girls on a canvas in a way that nobody but he could decipher, and a young couple walking down the road talking about the baby they were expecting.

What a beautiful day and what a beautiful moment I was having in that park, surrounded by the blue sky above and the grassy field all around! But, strangely, it was right at that moment, I mean, right at that refreshing, peaceful, shining moment, that a dark, gloomy, and deadening picture appeared to me. I didn't know where it came from, but it emerged right before my eyes and, in a second, the picture was so clear that I could see everything that was going on within it.

Please don't get me wrong. I was not in a lunatic ecstasy, but, as sure as I was standing there, I was seeing something I hadn't intended to see. In that doomed picture, everything I had been seeing, feeling, and enjoying in that peaceful park was overturned.

The shining grass became a bloody battlefield, the children throwing balls became soldiers throwing grenades, the sniffing dog became an armored tank, and the beautiful fountain springing up became a nuclear missile launching pad on the fiery ground.

I was so shocked that I couldn't move or say anything.

When the image faded, I asked myself: "Where did that horrifying image come from?"

Fortunately, it wasn't long before I got the answer. Those horrifying images came from what I had seen from various war reports from Iraq and Afghanistan. They were the exact images that the reporters in Iraq and Afghanistan brought to us from those battlefields every day.

Why do you think I had that doomed image of war when I was so enjoying the shining blue sky in a gorgeous park? That was my question, too, at that time. I couldn't answer back then.

But now I know why. The painful images of war appeared to me because the things in this world cannot be isolated from one another. Even the most beautiful parts of this world, like the gorgeous park I was in, do not stand alone. Everything is connected under one Creator we profess as God, so even the worst image on earth, like that of war, is part of what we see in the tight, universal unity of the world.

Even further, I have realized that it may be our heavy duty to remember the worst of the world even as we enjoy the best of the world, just as I did in that beautiful park.

But again, we might ask, "Why?"

Yes, it may be that everything in the universe may be united under one Creator and we have to remember the worst of the world as our heavy duty. We admit that. But, still, why? The question may be better stated as: why do we wage war, one of the most terrifying things we can imagine?

Some weeks ago, I was watching a television debate on the wars in Iraq and Afghanistan. The panelists were discussing the root causes of the two wars. One panelist said that religious and cultural conflict is the root cause of the wars. Another said that obtaining crude oil and political control over the Middle East is the key cause of the wars. And another said that it was religious extremism and international terrorism.

Finally, an enthusiastic caller, repeating Samuel Huntington's famous theory, said that it was simply the inevitable clash of civilizations. All of these possible answers and the careful analyses that led to them orbit around us all the time as we struggle to find the right answer. But, the problem is that no one is sure of the exact cause of wars, despite those wonderful analyses, because no single cause provokes any war.

However, in all those analyses we find one fundamental thing in common: human beings' weakness in moral behavior, and the corruption of their cultural or religious ideals against war. Put simply, we generally try to be moral and nonviolent in our ethical ideals and behavior, but we often fail in this attempt. And in our religious ideals, we also try to keep peace with one another, with other religions, and with people of different skin colors, cultures, nations, ethnicities, and genders, but we often find ourselves failing in that great religious pursuit as well.

I believe that this is why the words of former French President Jacques Chirac continue to echo in our ears. He said, "As far as I'm concerned, war always means failure." Therefore, is it any wonder that we continuously ask and pray to God to help us escape this great peril of human warfare? It seems no wonder to me because war means we have failed. We ask and pray to God today, just as Isaiah did, that nations "shall beat their swords into plowshares, and their spears into pruning hooks; [and] nation shall not lift up sword against nations neither shall they learn war anymore."

Isaiah fervently prayed so because he knew from his own experience the cruelty of war: torture, murder, maiming, disease, and merciless death! The horrible products of human warfare! Don't you know yourselves that what Isaiah knew and experienced is happening today in Iraq and Afghanistan? Sadly, already three hundred young Americans have fallen in Afghanistan this year alone. How terrible that is, and how we grieve for them and their families!

So, we pray just like Isaiah. "Please, good Lord, help us in this painful peril!" We pray that over and over and over again. We must!

And I hope, in that tearful prayer, we will be able to hear what Isaiah heard in his own prayer to God:

⁶ The wolf shall live with the lamb,

the leopard shall lie down with the kid,

the calf and the lion and the fatling together,

and a little child shall lead them.

⁷ The cow and the bear shall graze,

their young shall lie down together;

and the lion shall eat straw like the ox.

. . .

⁹ They will not hurt or destroy

on all my holy mountain;

for the earth will be full of the knowledge of the LORD

as the waters cover the sea. (Isa 11:6–7, 9)

A great message of hope, a liberating message of salvation, and the wonderful message of peace!

Do you yourself hear this hopeful message speaking to your heart from Scripture today? Do you hear this challenging message ringing from deep in your hearts in your own prayers to God? I believe when you do that God is speaking to your mourning hearts with this great news of hope, salvation, and peace.

I believe this great message of hope was what General McChrystal, the top commander in Afghanistan, had in his mind when he spoke on CBS's 60 Minutes. He said that we will need a totally different strategy in Afghanistan. So far, our chief strategy has been killing our enemies. But now, he said, we need a strategy that defeats violent factions by building relationships with and protecting the Afghan people and by focusing on developing a competent and honest government on which they can rely.

Do you hear what the general is saying to us? He wants us to beat our swords of destruction into the plowshares of reconstruction and turn our spears of killing and bombing into pruning hooks of peace, love, healing, and life. Or as Dr. King preached decades ago, we may have to actively love our enemies. That's the point. . . . That's the point.

Dorothy Thompson, the journalist expelled from Nazi Germany, once said, "Peace has to be created . . . It is the product of

Faith, Strength, Energy, Will, Sympathy, Justice, Imagination, and the triumph of Principle. It will never be achieved by passivity and quietism." She knew that peace is not just the absence of war and invited us to faithfully act for the peace and healing of the broken world, just as General McChrystal advocates that great proactive task of peace and love.

This is why I invite all of you as well to that special task of love and peace today, by doing whatever small things we can do now. Praying at home, writing letters to politicians, demonstrating (peacefully!) on the streets, joining and supporting anti-war groups, and, finally, most importantly, loving our enemies as ourselves.

When we do so all together in one mind and with one hope of peace, I believe the depressing vision I had at the park will be overturned again. The bloody battlefield will again become the shining, grassy field; the soldiers throwing grenades will again become the children throwing balls; the armored tank in the sandy desert will again become the peaceful dog sniffing around; and the nuclear missile launching pad on the fiery ground will again become the blessed fountain beautifully springing up—Isaiah's hopeful vision of peace and reconciliation!

I believe it.

Amen.

# Bibliography

*African American Heritage Hymnal*, 1st ed. Chicago: GIA, 2001.

Abbington, James. *Readings in African America Music and Worship*. Chicago: GIA, 2001.

Ansbro, John J. *Martin Luther King, Jr.: The Making of a Mind*. Maryknoll, NY: Orbis, 1982.

Baer, Hans, and Merrill Singer. *African American Religion: Varieties of Protest and Accommodation*. Knoxville: University of Tennessee Press, 2002.

Baldwin, Lewis V. *There is a Balm in Gilead: The Cultural Roots of Martin Luther King, Jr.* Minneapolis: Fortress, 1991.

Barth, Karl. *Revolutionary Theology in Making*. Translated by James D. Smart. Richmond: John Knox, 1964.

Bellah, N. Robert. *The Broken Covenant: American Civil Religion in Time of Trial*. New York: Seabury, 1975.

Binckes, Robin. *The Great Trek Uncut: Escape from British Rule: the Boer Exodus from the Cape Colony 1836*. Pinehill, ZA: 30° South, 2013

Bowne, Borden P. *Personalism*. New York: Houghton Mifflin, 1908.

Brightman, Edgar Sheffield. *Moral Laws*. New York: Abingdon, 1933.

Broderick, Francis L. and August Meier, eds. *Negro Protest Thought in the Twentieth Century*. New York: Bobbs-Merrill, 1965.

Bruegemann, Walter. *The Prophetic Imagination*. Minneapolis: Fortress, 2001.

Carson, Clayborne, and Peter Holloran, eds. *A Knock at Midnight: Inspiration from the Great Sermons of Reverend Martin Luther King, Jr.* New York: Intellectual Properties Management in association with Warner Books, 1998.

Carson, Clayborne, Ralph Luker, and Penny A. Russell, eds. *The Papers of Martin Luther King, Jr.* Berkeley: University of California Press, 1992.

Chandler, Daniel. *Semiotics: The Basics*. London; New York: Routledge, 2002.

Cilliers, Johan. *God for Us: An Analysis and Assessment of Dutch Reformed Preaching During the Apartheid Years*. Stellenbosch, ZA: Sun Press, 2006.

Cone, James H. *A Black Theology of Liberation*. Philadelphia: Lippincott, 1977.

———. *For My People: Black Theology and the Black Church*. Maryknoll, NY: Orbis, 1984.

———. *Martin & Malcolm & America: A Dream or a Nightmare.* Maryknoll, NY: Orbis, 1991.

———. *The Spirituals and the Blues: An Interpretation.* Maryknoll, NY: Orbis, 2000.

Craddock, Fred B. *Preaching.* Nashville: Abingdon, 1985.

Davis, George W. "The Ethical Basis of Christian Theology." *Crozer Quarterly* 16 (July 1939) 177–189.

DeWolf, Harold, ed. *A Theology of the Living Church.* New York: Harper & Row, 1960.

Erskine, Noel L. *King among the Theologians.* Cleveland: Pilgrim, 1994.

Garrow, David J. *Bearing the Cross: Martin Luther King Jr., and the Southern Christian Leadership Conference.* New York: Morrow, 1986.

———. *Martin Luther King, Jr.: Civil Rights Leader, Theologian, Orator.* Martin Luther King, Jr. And the Civil Rights Movement, Vols. 1–3. Brooklyn, NY: Carlson, 1989.

Hicks, H. Beecher, Jr. *Images of the Black Preacher: The Man Nobody Knows.* Valley Forge, PA: Judson, 1977.

Jones, Ilion T. *Principles and Practice.* Nashville: Abingdon, 1956.

King, Martin Luther, Jr. *The Measure of a Man.* Philadelphia: Fortress, 1988.

———. *The Papers of Martin Luther King, Jr.* 7 vols. Edited by Clayborne Carson. Berkeley: University of California Press, 1992–2014.

———. "The Rising Tide of Racial Consciousness." *The YWCA Magazine* (December 1960) 4–6.

———. *Strength to Love.* Philadelphia: Fortress, 1981.

———. *Stride toward Freedom: The Montgomery Story.* New York: Harper, 1958.

———. *The Trumpet of Conscience.* New York: Harper & Row, 1967.

———. "The UnChristian Christian." *Ebony* 20 (August 1965) 76–80.

Knudson, Albert C. *The Philosophy of Personalism.* New York: Abingdon, 1927.

Lakoff, George, and Mark Johnson. *Metaphors We Live By.* Chicago: University of Chicago Press, 2003.

LaRue, Cleophus J. *The Heart of Black Preaching.* Louisville: Westminster John Knox, 1999.

Lewis, David L. *King; A Critical Biography.* New York: Praeger, 1970.

Lincoln, C. Eric, and Lawrence H. Mamiya. *The Black Church in the African-American Experience.* Durham: Duke University Press, 1990.

Lischer, Richard. *The Preacher King: Martin Luther King Jr. and the Word that Moved America.* New York: Oxford University Press, 1995.

Livermore, Mary A. *My Story of the War: A Woman's Narrative of Four Years Personal Experience as Nurse in the Union Army, and in Relief Work at Home, in Hospitals, Camps, and at the Front During the War of Rebellion. With anecdotes, Pathetic Incidents and Thrilling Reminiscences Portraying the Lights and Shadows of Hospital Life and the Sanitary Service of the War.* Hartford, CT: Worthington 1889.

Long, Thomas G. *The Witness of Preaching.* Louisville: Westminster John Knox Press, 1989.

Mays, Benjamin E. *Disturbed About Man*. Richmond: John Knox, 1969.

———. *The Negro's God, as Reflected in His Literature*. New York: Negro Universities Press, 1969.

Mitchell, Henry H. *Black Preaching: The Recovery of a Powerful Art*. Nashville: Abingdon, 1990.

Moltmann, Jürgen. *Theology of Hope: On the Ground and the Implications of a Christian Eschatology*. New York: Harper & Row, 1967.

Muelder, Walter G. *Moral Law in Christian Social Ethics*. New York: Abingdon, 1943.

Oates, Stephen B. *Let the Trumpet Sound: The Life of Martin Luther King, Jr.* New York: New American Library, 1982.

Patte, Daniel. *The Cambridge Dictionary of Christianity*. New York: Cambridge University Press, 2010.

Proctor, Samuel D. *The Certain Sound of the Trumpet: Crafting a Sermon of Authority*. Valley Forge, PA: Judson, 1994.

Raboteau, Albert J. *A Fire in the Bones*. Boston: Beacon, 1995.

Sanster, W. E. *The Craft of the Sermon*. London: Epworth, 1954.

Smith, Kenneth L., and Ira G. Zepp. *Search for the Beloved Community: The Thinking of Martin Luther King, Jr.* Lanham, MD: University Press of America, 1986.

Southern, Eileen, and Josephine R. B. Wright, eds. *African-American Traditions in Song, Sermon, Tale, and Dance, 1600s–1920: An Annotated Bibliography of Literature, Collections, and Artworks*. New York: Greenwood, 1990.

Sweazey, George E. *Preaching the Good News*. Englewood Cliffs, NJ: Prentice-Hall, 1976.

Thurman, Howard. *Jesus and the Disinherited*. New York: Abingdon-Cokesbury, 1948.

Tillich, Paul. *The Shaking of the Foundations*. New York: Scribner, 1955.

———. *The Courage to Be*. 2nd ed., Yale Nota Bene. New Haven: Yale University Press, 2000.

Washington, James Melvin, ed. *A Testament of Hope: The Essential Writings and Speeches of Martin Luther King, Jr.* New York: HarperSanFrancisco, 1991.

Watley, William D. *Roots of Resistance: The Nonviolent Ethic of Martin Luther King, Jr.* Valley Forge, PA: Judson, 1985.

Wills, Richard W. *Martin Luther King Jr. and the Image of God*. New York: Oxford University Press, 2009.

Wilmore, Garyraud S., and James H. Cone. *Black Theology: A Documentary History*. Maryknoll, NY: Orbis, 1979.

White, Woodie W. "A Letter to Martin Luther King, Jr." The United Methodist Church Official Web-Site, https://rmnetwork.org/a-letter-to-dr-martin-luther-king-jr/.

Wink, Walter. *Engaging the Powers: Discernment and Resistance in a World of Domination*. Minneapolis: Fortress, 1992.

Woodson, Carter G., ed. *The Works of Francis J. Grimke, Volume 1: Addresses Mainly Personal and Racial*. Washington, DC: Associated Publishers, 1942.

# Subject Index

agape, 49, 54, 84

Baptist, 1, 5, 11, 11n20, 12, 29,
    36, 64n17, 68
Beloved/beloved community, 2,
    4, 10n13, 28n73, 48, 49,
    50, 86
Birmingham, 3, 33, 34, 35, 53
Black/black
    Christians, Christianity, 6,
        56, 60n3, 64, 64n17,
        65n18, 66, 67n24, 68,
        68n26
    church, xi, 2, 3, 5, 6, 6n6, 7,
        7n6, 8, 9, 13, 25, 27, 50,
        60, 60n4, 61, 62, 62n8,
        63n10 64n17, 65n18,
        67n24, 68n26, 69–70,
        76, 77, 80
    community, 13, 31, 33, 44,
        54, 62
    Exodus, 60n3, 65n18, 66, 68,
        70, 71
    people, 5, 12, 13, 15n32, 29,
        29n75, 30, 32, 34, 35,
        42, 44, 45, 56, 66–70, 72,
        79, 83
    theology, 10, 13, 13n25,
        13n27, 14, 15, 15n31,
        15n32, 16, 44
Boston University, 3, 9, 11n18,
    18, 20, 22, 23

capitalist (capitalism), 68, 82
civil rights, x, 1, 6n6, 7n6, 8, 9,
    13n25, 15, 18, 20, 23,
    29n75, 31, 34, 35, 42, 57,
    65n18, 73, 78, 83
    act of 1964, 57, 83
colonialism, 69
cosmic
    God, 39
    liberation, 50
Crozer Seminary, 3, 9, 11n18,
    18–21, 21n49

dream, 17, 28n73, 35, 36, 49, 53,
    74, 85, 86

Ebenezer church, 9, 11n20, 12
Emancipation Proclamation,
    57, 83
Emory University, 85
eschatology (eschatological), 6,
    12, 28n73, 45, 48, 49, 52,
    57, 60, 82
evil, 3, 4, 26, 27, 39, 40, 45–47,
    47n22, 49, 51, 53, 55–58,
    60, 63, 65, 67, 67n23, 69,
    70–75, 75n36, 77
Exodus, 56, 59–60, 60n3, 61, 62,
    62n8 65, 65n18, 66, 67,
    67n24, 68, 68n26, 69–77

# Name Index

Barth, Karl, 3, 9, 23, 25–27
Cone, James H., 10, 12, 13,
    14n29, 15, 15n31,
    15n32, 44, 45, 51, 51n35,
    52n35
Craddock, Fred B., 63, 64
Davis, George Washington, 9,
    19, 19n41, 47n23
DeWolf, Harold, 9, 20, 22
Erskine, Noel L., 10, 15, 25
Gandhi, Mohandas, K., 29, 31,
    32
Grimke, Francis J., 66
Huntington, Samuel, 89
Jefferson, Thomas, 56, 83
LaRue, Cleophus James, 61
Lincoln, Abraham, 56, 57,
    64n17, 83
Lischer, Richard, 8–12, 16, 74
Long, Thomas G., 63, 64

Mays, Benjamin E., 9, 16–18,
    67n24
McChrystal, Stanley A.
    (General), 91
Moltmann, Jürgen, 82
Muhammad, Elijah, 34
Parks, Rosa, 31, 53, 54
Raboteau, Albert J., 60, 60n3,
    65n18
Rauschenbusch, Watler, 31, 32
Thompson, Dorothy, 91
Thoreau, Henry David, 30
Tillich, Paul, 3, 9, 23–25, 27,
    47n23
Truth, Sojourner, 83
White, Woodie W. (Bishop),
    85–86
Wieman, Henry Nelson, 23
Wink, Walter, 45–47, 78

Made in the USA
Monee, IL
18 February 2020